Contemporary Yugoslav Poetry

IOWA TRANSLATIONS

Contemporary Korean Poetry
Modern Chinese Poetry
Mihail Eminescu
The Poetry of Postwar Japan
Contemporary Yugoslav Poetry

GENERAL EDITORS

Paul Engle
Hualing Nieh Engle

Contemporary Yugoslav Poetry

EDITED BY

Vasa D. Mihailovich

 UNIVERSITY OF IOWA PRESS   IOWA CITY

The translation of *Hunting, The Foundling , The Chorus of Dogs in Knossos, The Blind King in Exile,* and *The Conqueror in Constantinople* are copyright 1969 and 1976 by Joachim Neugroschel, and are reprinted with his permission.

The New River Press also grants permission for the use of translations of Ivan V. Lalić's poems which appeared in *Fire Gardens* (1971).

Library of Congress Cataloging in Publication Data

Main entry under title:

Contemporary Yugoslav poetry.

    (Iowa translations)
    1. Yugoslav poetry—Translations into English.
2. English poetry—Translations from Southern Slavic languages.   I. Mihailovich, Vasa D. II. Series.
PG584.E3C6   891.8'2'15   77-22865
ISBN 0-87745-077-3
ISBN 0-87745-080-3 pbk.

University of Iowa Press, Iowa City   52242
© 1977 by The University of Iowa. All rights reserved
Printed in the United States of America

Foreword

Theology once believed that "translation" could mean direct removal to heaven of the body without intervening death. All too often in being translated, the poem loses its life.

Literal translation of a poem into bare prose may help understanding, but the plain text of a literal version may not be accurate to the poem, for what a poet writes is not a literal account of his life, but an imaginative vision of it. Only a translator with imagination can truly translate the imaginative language of a poem.

The Iowa Translations series is an expression of the International Writing Program, which brings writers from all parts of the world to the University of Iowa to write, to know each other, and to translate. We believe that in the hazardous twentieth century men of good mind and good will must talk to each other or die. We believe that poetry is the highest form of talk, and that translating it is therefore an honor and a privilege, as well as one of the toughest jobs known to man.

One of the most attractive qualities of contemporary Yugoslav poetry is its lyrical and symbolic use of the concrete details of daily life. Stevan Raičković writes that "an ant on my knee is like a man on a hill." Miodrag Pavlović says that "The dawn already wiggles under the pillow." Vasko Popa writes in his long series about the little box, "Throw into the little box / A mouse / You'll take out a shaking hill." In the title poem beginning the sequence he says:

And she grows bigger bigger bigger
Now the room is inside her
And the house and the city and the earth
And the world she was in before

The little box remembers her childhood
And by a great great longing
She becomes a little box again

Now in the little box
You have the whole world in miniature
You can easily put it in a pocket
Easily steal it easily lose it

Take care of the little box

Bogomil Gjuzel's poem "Professional Poet" reminds one of the desperate Japanese writer who committed suicide because he could no longer bear the sight of the empty page. It concludes:

Back to the module:
            Daddy, what does it mean
to be a monster? Suddenly the chain of command dissolves
bits of paper whirling in free fall
around the table:
                  untouched paper
and your pencil, ominous as a revolver.

(Tr. Carolyn Kizer)

Any darkness in these poems has been earned; it is the true color that follows fire. It is astonishing, after the Nazi occupation, the constant fighting, the blood on street, field, and mountain, the imposed poverty of the war, that such a richness of poetry should be created. These are tough poets, who lived with death as luckier parts of the world lived with sunlight. It was a daily fact, visible to the eye. From conditions out of which many people made self-pity, they made the art of poetry in Macedonian, Slovenian, and Serbo-Croatian words. They honored the life-experience. It is an honor to translate them.

Paul Engle and *Hualing Nieh Engle*
Directors, International Writing Program
School of Letters, The University of Iowa

Preface

Some of these poems have previously appeared in the following publications, to whose editors grateful acknowledgment is made: *The Bridge, Extension, Edge, The Literary Review, Lillabulero, The Minnesota Review, Modern Poetry in Translation, Mundus Artium, Dragonfly, The Stony Brook, Sumac, Work.*

Gratitude is also expressed to all translators for permission to publish their work.

Special gratitude goes to Charles Simic, whose untiring contribution to the anthology is largely responsible for its quality.

The anthology covers a wide spectrum of contemporary Yugoslav poets, from those who started publishing before World War II to the very recent ones, with the bulk representing the middle generation, which is now the most active group on the Yugoslav poetry scene.

The authors are presented in the order of their appearance as poets. The editor rejects any claim to completeness or an even distribution among the many nationalities of Yugoslavia. The selection of poets and poems was governed exclusively by their quality and availability of translation. Some poets have declined permission to be included in this anthology.

The introduction was written by a scholar not associated with editing the anthology, and the editor expresses his warmest thanks to her.

General Editors' Acknowledgments

Special thanks are due the Northwest Area Foundation of Saint Paul, Minnesota (John D. Taylor, executive director, A. A. Heckman, former executive director) for its generous grant to the International Writing Program in support of translation. This fund has helped talented young American writers work with foreign writers in the "co-translation" of many texts. One of the Foundation's purposes is "To aid in development of new bodies of knowledge." It is a purpose of this Program to bring into English new bodies of the literary imagination and to give a fresh knowledge of poetry in languages which have been little translated.

The Ford Foundation (Richard Sheldon) helped bring many writers from East Europe to the Program, including several from Yugoslavia.

Many Foundations, private individuals and corporations have contributed funds which helped make this Program possible, including the present volume. We are continually surprised at the good will of business men toward writers from the far corners of the world.

The American Embassy in Belgrade has steadily contributed to the costs of sending brilliant writers from Yugoslavia to the International Writing Program. This book is a small return for their assistance.

Many have helped from the Department of State. John Richardson, Jr., assistant secretary of state, Bureau of Educational and Cultural Affairs, has always been sympathetic and perceptive, as have many working in the cultural area in the Department.

The University of Iowa has long been an innovative patron of all the arts. In now offering a Master of Fine Arts in Translation degree, it recognizes that translating is not simply a craft, but an art of its own. Willard L. Boyd, president of the University, has given constant support.

One of many who have helped the International Writing Program, Robert Yaw, president, Souvenir, Inc., Cedar Rapids, Iowa, has given his personal time and his practical experience.

The Writers Unions of Slovenia, Croatia, and Serbia were very hospitable on our trip to Yugoslavia, where we met many of these poets in an atmosphere of openness and freedom.

Paul Engle and *Hualing Nieh Engle*

Gertrud Graubert Champe

The Poetry of Postwar Yugoslavia

The poetries existing in Yugoslavia since 1946 are one and yet not one: sprung from different origins, each grew almost alone for a thousand years until the federation took place which formed today's Yugoslavia. From that time on, the problems and privileges of poets have been largely the same in all the republics, and so have many of the large aspirations. The difference between the languages and poetries of the republics is taken as a self-evident starting point by the poets of Yugoslavia, but bears some description for outsiders.

The state of Yugoslavia is a federation of six republics: Bosnia and Hercegovina, Croatia, Macedonia, Montenegro, Serbia, and Slovenia. The federation also includes two autonomous enclaves within the Republic of Serbia, which have been given special status because of their particular history and population. These are Vojvodina, which has a large Hungarian population, and Kosovo, inhabited largely by people of Albanian descent. The approximately twenty-one million inhabitants of the federation fall into six groups, essentially ethnic, which are designated nations: Serbs, Croats, Moslems, Slovenes, Macedonians, and Montenegrins.

The chief language of Yugoslavia, spoken by Croats, Montenegrins, Moslems, and Serbs, is officially designated as Serbo-Croatian in Serbia and Croato-Serbian in Croatia. The hyphenated name is a graphic representation of the tendency of this language to pull apart into two separate entities, corresponding roughly to the eastern and the western usage, namely Serbian and Croatian. This tendency is alive both in the spoken and the written languages. There are also 1.7 million speakers of Slovene, 1.5 million speakers of Macedonian, and one million speakers of Albanian in Yugoslavia.

The languages of Yugoslavia are distributed across the country in a graduated spectrum rather than as discontinuous entitites. This distribution can be verified on a linguistic basis, but also through the folklore and oral poetry, which do not change abruptly at national boundaries. These languages result from independent developments and modifications of a language which is thought to have been common to the Slavic tribes moving south and westward across the Carpathian mountains in the fifth and sixth centuries A.D. Each of the South Slavic nations came to literacy in its own language through the same medium—the written language devised by the Eastern missionaries Cyril and Methodius for the purpose of bringing the Christian Scriptures to all the Slavs. This language, now called Old Church Slavic, began to be disseminated around the middle of the ninth century. It was based on a Macedonian dialect, first written in an alphabet called glagolitic, and then in the Greek-based Cyrilic alphabet which is still used by Eastern Slavs today.

At first, Old Church Slavic was comprehensible to all Slavs. It remained homogeneous for over a hundred years, and then began to assimilate characteristics of languages spoken in each region where it was used, so that by the end of the eleventh century, it is possible to distinguish between an Old Church Slavic manuscript in a Serbian recension and a manuscript in a Croatian recension. By the end of the thirteenth century, the assimilation of the vernacular into the church language had gone so far is some regions that one can already speak of vernacular literary languages. This process occurred more rapidly in Catholic Slovenia and Croatia than in Orthodox Serbia and Macedonia.

From the Middle Ages to the nineteenth century, the development of literary languages based on the vernacular was now impeded, now influenced by the proximity of an overwhelming outside power, be it a church or a neighboring state with expansionist designs on the territory. The suppression of national culture was often so consistent and so relentless that in reaction, a linguistic act has long been considered a political act, so intended and so perceived.

Although the development of literature in each republic is amply described in literary histories, it is of interest to note here the dynamics of this development, which sometimes still marks the poetry being written today.

Serbian literature, written in Old Church Slavic, was independent and fruitful during the early Middle Ages. After the Turks gained a major stronghold in Serbia in 1389, literature, sheltered by a decimated Orthodox Church, took on a popular, folkloristic coloration. In the late seventeenth and early eighteenth centuries, Serbian literature underwent a strong influence from Russia and became an ornate and rarefied phenomenon, infinitely remote from the spoken language of the people. The influence of Russia was broken by Austrian intervention in the second half of the eighteenth century, but Austrian influence also resulted in estrangement between the written and the spoken languages, an estrangement that was actively fostered by the Serbian Orthodox Church, both at home and among Serbian scholars abroad. Most of the credit for returning the Serbian language to the people is usually given to the philologist Vuk Stefanović Karadzić (1787–1864). It was he who urged the adoption of a single dialect by all people who spoke a mutually understandable language. The dialect he chose for this purpose was one noted for its exceptional clarity, spoken in Hercegovina, midway between the two largest nations affected by his efforts. The basis of Vuk's arguments and demonstrations in favor of a single written language was the folklore of Serbia, Croatia, and all the regions between, of which he was a pioneering collector. This collection is probably Vuk's greatest contribution, since it continues to nourish poets to this day.

Modern written Slovene arose during the Reformation, when for the first time Slovenia had the possibility of enjoying its own language publicly. The first great translator of the Scriptures into Slovene was Bishop Primoz Trubar, and his linguistic efforts became a symbol of unity to a nation which had been forced in the past to carry on its intellectual life in Latin, German, and Italian. Trubar's work survived the counter-Reformation and was vigorously defended by poets and intellectuals at critical moments of choice. On the one hand, Slovenes refused to give in to Pan-Slavic sentiments which called for translation of the Scriptures into some language intelligible to all Slavs. On the other hand, later writers resisted the strong local patriotisms which yearned for several distinct forms of literary Slovene reflecting the spoken languages of various regions. Nor were writers willing to abandon their own growing literature in order to gain a wider audience by forming a linguistic union with Croatia.

The repeated decision to maintain a single, independent literary Slovene probably sprang mainly from a need to preserve a Slavic identity in spite of the strong political and intellectual influence of neighboring Austria.

Croatia began its path to linguistic independence by wresting from the Roman Catholic Church the right to worship in a Slavic language. Once the obligatory tie to Latin had been severed in 1201, a literary Croatian began to grow rapidly, especially in the Dalmatian coastal regions. The young language fed on the translation of Latin manuscripts, the incorporation of folk motifs, and later, on the influence of the Italian Renaissance as transmitted by Venice. When the center of literary activity shifted northward in the seventeenth century, the tendency at first was for scholars to write in Latin. However, the use of Croatian rather than Latin soon became the rule, signaling an intention to retain an identity, in spite of Austro-Hungarian pressures to the contrary. In the nineteenth century, there were Croatian men of letters who felt, like Karadžic in Serbia, the need to increase the strength of the language by declaring solidarity with all speakers of mutually understandable dialects. In this spirit, Croatian was normalized upon one of its most Eastern dialects, through the efforts of scholars such as Ljudevit Gaj. A linguistic agreement between Serbia and Croatia was signed at Vienna in 1850, declaring the languages one.

The literary language of Bosnia and Hercegovina is Serbo-Croatian, and yet it presents a separate history of linguistic development. Its literary situation is of great interest. Lying on the boundary of two worlds, close to the line which once separated the Western from the Eastern Roman Empire, Bosnia-Hercegovina has chosen to see its diversity as a strength rather than as a force for disorder. The literature embraces Serbian, Croatian, and Moslem traditions, and is deepened and embellished by a fascination with the Bogumils, a medieval heretic sect once powerful in Bosnia. In other words, Bosnia-Hercegovina sees itself a living expression of the capacity for coexistence which is held up as the Yugoslav ideal.

Macedonian linguistic and literary development were severely restricted until after World War II. Once the cradle of Slavic literacy, Macedonia became, still in the Middle Ages, a land with a proscribed native language. This suppression was due largely to the activities of the Greek Orthodox Church, and had to do not only with religious, but also with territorial expansionism. Concerted efforts to achieve the public and official use of Macedonian began in the eighteenth century, but as late as the early twentieth century, during the Yugoslav Kingdom, the public use of Macedonian was forbidden. After 1945, great federal support was given to the development of a literary Macedonian, and it remains a task in which poets and scholars are actively engaged.

Throughout the history of the South Slavic nations, the urge for an independent language has been closely connected with the urge for national self-determination. Although these movements encourage and reinforce each other productively, the combination of the two can also lead into unproductive, anti-literary byways. The Croatian poet, critic, and musician A. G. Matoš, who lived both in Zagreb and in Belgrade, was acutely aware of this problem and wrote some of his most eloquent essays in an attempt to arouse the decent pride of his countrymen, so that they would fall prey neither to slavish imitation of the West nor to the paranoia of provincial nationalism. His analysis of the relationship between the health of a nation and the vigor of its literature is a classic of public criticism.

Always, in the South Slavic nations, the most convincing advances toward a living independence have been made through poetry. Indeed, there have been periods when only the poet was able to express with accuracy and impunity the nation's painful and hopeful sense of itself. This has given a special status to the poet in Yugoslavia which he retains today in a much wider sector of the population than might be expected.

II *Literature and Politics*

A survey of the relationship between poets and government is essential for characterizing the postwar poetry of Yugoslavia. Among the Communist nations of Eastern Europe, Yugoslavia is unique in not resigning itself helplessly to a literature rigidly dominated by commisars. The freedom available to a Yugoslav poet is by no means equal to the atmosphere in which a Western poet functions, but there has always been found a brave man here and there willing to keep hammering at the brick wall of literary commitment by legislation from above. It must also be pointed out that the government itself has occasionally made efforts to move away from the rigid literary policy typical of the Soviet Union. That reform has failed is perhaps a necessary consequence of what Communist theory has to say about the role of literature in society. The fact remains that literary freedom is a condition which can be discussed in Yugoslavia, a concept with some meaning.

At the end of World War II and with the triumph of the socialist revolution in Yugoslavia, all the nations whose literary development has been shown to be separate were brought into a federation. In each of the republics, a new branch of literature began to develop, often at the expense of the flourishing literature which had existed before the war. The new growth proceeded under conditions which were rather uniform for the whole country; it depended to a large extent upon the special relationship between the writer and the government which obtains in a socialist state.

For Yugoslavia, this relationship had its roots in the 1920s, with the appearance of a literary avant garde which published in the leftist press and presumably spoke for the Communist party of Yugoslavia. Although a "normal" literary life was going on in Yugoslavia between the wars, filled with experimentation and inspiration ranging from personal lyricism through social protest to patriotic effusions, the voice of the avant garde became more strident as the Communist party gained in strength. Since many of the members of the avant garde came to power in the new Yugoslavia and determined its literary policy, it is their behavior which we must follow here. The leftist writers repeatedly and unequivocally declared talent to be less important than a social perspective, and with great pathos, dubbed literature the faithful servant of the revolution. The terms used to characterize opponents of this view of literature were hardly literary and not at all original: formalist, decadent, bourgeois lackey, and fascist.

The position of literature in society seemed clear-cut to Marxist ideologues, but the situation was in fact ambiguous and turbulent for practicing poets of the time. One of the first groups to be confronted by the growing young party's literary dicta was the circle of surrealist poets centered in Belgrade. These writers, strongly influenced by the surrealist movement in France, were searching for ways to introduce the revolution into their own writing. As a group, they were vociferous critics of the social order they saw around them, but their methods could not live side by side with those of the hard-core party writers who were already committed in 1932 to a type of realism which became programmatic in 1934.

The surrealists' group dissolved under the weight of a humorless, a-literary polemic when it was unable to counter aggressive dogmatism with an equally intense solidarity of its own. Some of the members, such as Aleksandar Vučo, Djordje Jovanović, and Oskar Davičo, joined the movement of social literature. They spoke through the periodical *Naša stvarnost* (Our Reality) and were basically influenced by the Communist party. Others, like Marko Ristić and Miroslav Krleža, withdrew to found the journal *Danas* (Today) and later, in 1939, *Pečat* (The Seal). These writers and their followers were leftist intellectuals, but leftists who insisted that they could only perform as independent individuals. Claiming that each writer is solely responsible for finding his own effective relationship between literature and society, they made the struggle between the artists and society quite public, and gave a sharp definition to the area in which the battle would be fought.

The most visible, persistent, and articulate personality in modern Yugoslavia's fight for a literature worth writing and reading has been Miroslav Krleža. Paradoxically, this prolific novelist, poet, and dramatist has captured the minds of readers for a good part of the twentieth century with a theme which is less than current: the decadence of the Austro-Hungarian ruling class as it concerns their eastern provinces. His indisputable social concern and striving for sensitivity to the times are in fact best reflected in his theoretical writings and public utterances from the thirties to the present. The main steps in the carving out of a literary space in Yugoslavia can be traced through articles and speeches of his.

By 1933, Krleža had already published much, and was generally considered an outstanding writer, admired not only for his talent but also for his commitment to the battle against the bourgeois social mentality. At this stage in his career, he wrote a twenty-page introduction to a book of drawings by Krsto Hegedušić, *Scenes from the Podravina*. The essay was a statement of his position in the conflict between the artist and the Party critic, an elucidation of the function of literature in society–the author indeed does have an obligation to society and even to the leftist movement, but has a prior and ineluctible obligation as an artist: to be himself. Literature, in Krleža's estimation, cannot be willed; it can neither be commanded from within nor from without. Krleža's ardent but essentially loyal plea for the affirmation of talent over mediocrity and originality over conformity called forth strong attacks from Milovan Djilas and from Radovan Zogović, who must be remembered for his merciless persecution of any form of art not dedicated to the glorification of the Party. Tito also came to the attack in an article entitled "Trotskyism and its Helpers."

Krleza's response was a lengthy treatise published in his journal *Pecat*, entitled "The Dialectical Antibarbarus." This work makes what should have been an annihilating attack on the far left wing of the Party for its barbaric denial of "man's totality," a denial implemented by slander, a malevolent use of any means to achieve its ends, and total deafness to dissenting views. Krleža was condemned outright by the highest Party leaders: Djilas, Kardelj, Tito. The Party was on the brink of a fateful struggle and no hearing would be given to a heretic. In 1940, Krleža's journal ceased publication and he himself sank into a silence which remained almost complete until 1952.

During the Second World War, the ancient, vexed question of whether literature shall instruct or delight remained at rest. An urgent need was felt among the leaders of the Partisan movement for material to encourage and inspire the population, both civilian and military. Many leftist writers who had resisted a totally committed literature became involved in war journalism and in the writing of stories and poems which were often read aloud to soldiers near the battlefield. This was a time of Partisan poetry, return to epic motifs and meters from the national oral poetry; a violently graphic quality, often learned from surrealism, marked much of the verse.

The Partisan war literature was the seed of the new literary growth in all the republics. Non-Partisan writers and anti-unification writers, or writers with avowed religious affiliation were silenced, at least for the time being. The literary life of Yugoslavia from 1945 to 1948 was firmly in the grip of socialist realism, Soviet style. It is true that some valuable texts were published during this time, such as three novels by Andrić, but this is work that was done in isolation during the war. The dominant literary voice of this time came from the "pickaxe and spade" writers, who sang of a nation trying to build and rebuild itself. There is no reason why this, of itself, should be a contemptible theme for literature. What is disheartening about the period, however, is the fact that any direction in writing other than the "literature of enthusiasm" was officially deprecated. At the First Congress of the Yugoslav Writers Union in 1946, Radovan Zogović spoke forcefully of the debt owed by the writers to the fighting and working citizenry; their task was to produce a gallant picture of these heroes, inspiring enough to spur the nation to even greater efforts. Indulgence in "personal lyricism" was tantamount to denial of the task. This charge was leveled, for instance, at the poetess Vesna Parun upon the appearance of *Zore i vihori* (Dawns and Gales); her songs of love and nature were not considered to be of use to anyone.

In 1948, Yugoslavia was expelled from the Cominform for repeated failure to comply with Soviet directives. This breach with Stalinism left the country isolated from both East and West and necessitated a rebuilding much more demanding than the constructing of railroads, highways, and factories. Withdrawal from the Soviet mold was slow and difficult. Stanko Lasić, an historian of the period as it concerns literature, wrote of it: ". . . the Yugoslav Communist movement began ridding itself of its theological structure, but it was not yet ready for the human structure." Those suspected of Stalinism were imprisoned, but the emptineess they left behind was not readily filled. At the Second Congress of the Yugoslav Writers Union in 1949, Krleža and Petar Šegedin both spoke of the necessity of a writer's commitment to the Left, but each man also asserted that a writer has a duty to be true to himself. These self-neutralizing statements did very little to encourage a new kind of writing, and the literary situation remained generally as it had been in 1945; most of the new works printed were written by former Partisans, the work of some older poets was collected and reprinted, anthologies were prepared, and critical discussions centered largely on the problems of an honorable and truthful representation of the Yugoslav socialist reality.

It is generally held that the year 1952 marks the start of a vigorous upswing in Yugoslav letters. The change was encouraged by a passage of time since the break with Stalinism and by the very real effort of Yugoslavia's men of letters to rid themselves of socialist realism. A good measure of the credit, however, must go specifically to an address by Miroslav Krleža at the Third Congress of the Yugoslav Writers Union (1952) entitled "On the Freedom of Culture." This speech contains a few bold points. One serves notice on the cultural establishments of the West that Yugoslavia will no longer tolerate the usual pitying, patronizing treatment. Communism, said Krleža, is far from being the domain of a barbaric, godless Asia. It is, in fact, a creation of the clear-eyed, civilized West, and Yugoslav socialism is a very Western application of this European creation. In a manner which has been characteristic of Yugoslav criticism since the nineteenth century, Krleža states that much of the difference between the Western cultural achievement and that of Yugoslavia (and he is pleased indeed to be able to say that there is some), is due to the fact that the West was able to build its culture in peace and prosperity while a country like Yugoslavia had to expend most of its energy simply to survive the encroachments of that same West.

Returning his attention to his own country, Krleza demonstrated without timidity that nothing in the cultural sphere could be more offensively anti-Marxist than socialist realism. The literature for which he calls instead is to be significantly more noble and more rational, but to most western literary sensibilities it must seem curiously related to the system he rejected with such contempt. If one takes Krleža at his word, his ideal literature was still to be monolithic in inspiration, even though a certain variety in execution would be held acceptable. It was definitely to be materialistic, and it was to eschew the frivolity of postwar survivals of modernism. By no means was the new Yugoslav literature to yearn toward the West as toward some brilliant and more fortunate older brother. Rather, without excessive nationalism or narrow regionalism, it was to take as its goal, theme, and formative genius the independent path toward socialism of the Federation of Yugoslavia. To fulfill these high expectations, it would have to be produced by writers with enough talent to give subjective expression to the concrete aspirations of the Yugoslav "leftist reality."

Krleža's speech must have made stirring listening compared to the fare at the first two Writers Congresses, offering as it did new perspectives of freer conditions. It did not, however, provide for a truly secure future. Although it delivered the poet from the tender ministrations of direct government censorship, it perpetuated the principle that there is and ought to be such a close relationship between literature and the health of the state that the state has the right to expect a certain kind of performance.

Whatever the force of Krleža's address might have been, there followed a period of increased literary activity as direct state control gradually began to recede, in accordance with the country's ideal vision of self-government in every facet of social endeavor. But militating against the new literary freedom was the growth of a bureaucracy of whom Milovan Djilas wrote in *The New Class:* "The world has seen few heroes as ready to sacrifice and suffer as the Communists were on the eve of and during the Revolution. It has probably never seen such characterless wretches and stupid defenders of arid formulae as they became after attaining power." The politicians and ideologues of this bureaucracy, however, still had the last word concerning the country's literature.

In confrontation with the bureaucracy, the writers took up a literary stance and program which has been called "socialist aestheticism." This term, by no means complimentary or even neutral, has been coined by Sveta Lukić, whose work, *Contemporary Yugoslav Literature,* attempts to analyze the events and structures contributing to the nature of postwar literature. According to Lukić, socialist aestheticism is the tendency, very visible in Yugoslav letters, to exclude the events of the immediately surrounding world from literature. It is presented as something of a cross between escape literature and the Formalist- New Critical stance. The fact that Lukić has isolated this phenomenon is not as informative as the manner in which he has done so.

In describing the situation out of which socialist realism arises, Lukić states that under socialism, the writer can for the first time say "yes" to his society. But according to Krleza, literature is the result of the writer's clash with society. If we incautiously combine the two statements, we must conclude that no literature is possible under socialism. This is the specter haunting those many poets who, in writing, explore the beautiful, soothing, but finally impossible alternative of not writing. And Lukić continues to incapacitate the exposition of his own argument when he labels the literary direction of the fifties and sixties *socialist* aestheticism. By this, he presumably intends to make a neat parallel with socialist realism. But the word *socialist* in the earlier term has not the same hopeful ring as in the later. Socialist realism is a positive phenomenon, expected to implement the ideology with which it is imbued. Socialist aestheticism is a dangerously negative consequence of the unpredictable forces in socialism.

Lukić's term is not a happy choice, but his message is clear: he and others before him have long wanted Yugoslavia's writers to examine their society critically, and in effect, to introduce a more discursive, moralistic tone into literature. But one difficulty of grappling with the contemporary world rather than evading it has been pointed out by no less a committed writer than Krleza. In a series of published interviews, *Conversations With Miroslav Krleža* (1969), he mused:

> How beautiful was socialism under capitalism, [when] all the blame [could] be laid conveniently on the capitalist system. But who is to be blamed under socialism, where men also suffer from toothache, illegitimate children are born, and where in a general way, people are also more or less petty, nervous, mean, ailing and poorly paid, trying to knife one another in every walk of life?

Lukić hurled his accusations at the writers without considering the possibility that there might exist a very real impediment to the "responsible" functioning. He says that they ignored what he calls "contemporary reality" simply so that they might avoid the possible wrath of the bureaucracy (which may not have been functioning responsibly itself.) But in socialist terms, this amounts to accusing them of placating the class enemy, and that is a strong accusation indeed. The poets have always answered it by saying, "We are not, after all, sociologists."

During the early postwar years, there was a great deal of pressure on poets to concern themselves with themes of sacrifice and reconstruction. Failure to comply with this pressure resulted largely in some kind of economic sanction, which was very easy to apply because almost all aspects of publishing, as well as the paternalistic Writers Unions, are to some extent controlled and financed by the government. The same kinds of sanctions are generally enforced when a writer utters too much rather than too little.

In spite of a policy, enunciated immediately after the end of World War II, of limited government intervention in cultural affairs, there are certain types of statement that can make a writer liable to official attention. Clearly, an author will be censured if he publishes anything affecting the country's foreign relations. In spite of the rupture of 1948, or perhaps because of it, this means essentially that he may not utter sentiments excessively antagonistic to the Soviet Union. Nor may he belittle the achievements of the People's Revolution in any way. Because of this, it can be dangerous to attempt the creation of structures implicitly called for in socialist theory. For instance, in the early fifties, several literary journals were founded in an effort to comply with young Marx's call for interdisciplinary exchange and for a platform for workers to speak on intellectual matters. Among these were *Delo* (The Work) in Belgrade, *Beseda* (The Word) and *Perspektive* (Perspectives) in Ljubljana, and *Krugovi* (Circles) in Zagreb. These and several other journals were known for their open discussions, uninhibited by considerations of bureaucratic displeasure. *Delo* is one of the very few survivors.

Another type of literary expression which is forbidden, because it threatens the brotherhood achieved by the Revolution, is that of strong nationalism within a republic of the federation. The struggle of nationalities is, understandably, carried out chiefly between the Serbs and the Croats. The Slovenes, by virtue of their separate language, are relatively free to go their own way culturally, and being the most prosperous of the republics, are not so dependent on central funds. Macedonia is also isolated from the struggle, but it has been found politically expedient to support the cultural individuality of this republic bordering on a watchful

Bulgaria. The real tension is among groups of that great majority of Yugoslavs who speak some variant of the language officially designated as Serbo-Croatian. These variants can clearly be localized geographically; like Churchill's proverbial Englishman, every member of the Serbo-Croatian language group receives a brand on his tongue the day he is born that sometimes identifies his nationality and always his region. The personal loyalty and emotional response evoked by a man's native speech is a rich substrate for a living folklore, for poetry and for a sense of cultural identity; it cannot be passed over with impunity.

But the state has other needs and interests and there have been attempts to arrive at agreements which would bring the usage of Serbs and Croats closer together, at least for public official purposes. To this end, a public agreement was forged in 1954, but it was honored mostly by being violated from the moment of its signing. This agreement has had repercussions which have not yet died out, almost twenty-five years later.

At issue is the language of instruction in the schools, the language to be used in television transmission in each of the republics, in the army, in official documents. The argument is all the more difficult since the differences between Serbian and Croatian have been very small since the nineteenth century, when each of the two republics chose a rather peripheral dialect as a norm for the sake of inter-republican uniformity. The factor which distinguishes the two languages most sharply is neither grammar nor lexicon, but cultural content. This fact, which has been lucidly explained by the philologist Radoslav Katičić, will have to be dealt with before a viable solution to the Yugoslav language controversy can be reached.

If a sweeping statement concerning poetic freedom in postwar Yugoslavia is to be attempted, it must include the fact that the state has always recognized the need for artistic freedom; this is clear from Tito's programmatic statements during the early years. The agonizing difficulty has been to find a way for this freedom to coexist with what were considered to be the needs of a new and struggling nation. There was great, sometimes intolerable pressure on the poets of Yugoslavia to produce a literature which was elevating, didactic, and even panegyric, and many poets did indeed comply with the letter of the government's demand. There were other poets who did not reject the didactic and panegyric but combined them with questioning and applied them to the inner life of man. These are the poets who are collected here.

The Poems

The poets represented in this collection are all people who were aware, to some degree, of the demands, promises, challenges, and dangers of the period overlapping with the end of World War II, during which Yugoslavia was becoming a Socialist Federated Republic. These poets were writing, or learning to write in a time when the intellectuals of Yugoslavia were alternately hammering out and waiting out the formation of a new relationship between the government and the poet. Almost all older than forty today, they stand as a group because their life or death as poets was largely being decided before their eyes by public events to which they could only react after the fact. It is their reaction which brings them together.

In a time when most poetry named the Revolution, decribed it and praised it, these poets seem to have ignored it. The name of the process which, according to the leaders, had changed their daily reality absolutely, is missing from the poems presented here. But if the poets do not name the Revolution, they do something more basic and interesting. They examine in all its consequences some strong but nameless lens through which the whole world comes to them. Is it the Revolution, is it the postwar twentieth century, or some other discontinuity in human existence? That is for them to sing and for us to search out.

From the poetry of postwar Yugoslavia rises a voice that cannot be ignored. "Now!" some poets cry, "Now!" others whisper, "it is time for us to be heard." Much of the clamor and unrest spring from the now-familiar dislocations of modernism which the bravest of the poets embraced in spite of official condemnation. Nature is made strange, man is made strange, and life becomes a sea of uneasiness. But the resulting poetry is not one of alienation and introspection; rather, its force is both didactic and questioning. Sometimes, the poet seems to be addressing his own nation only. Thus, Vlado Gotovac speaks of the obstacles the poet must overcome as a personal struggle:

> I, a skillful climber
> on a perfect top of a steeple
> which alone does not repeat
> a game that is already over,
> have placed a stone

with an invented name
in a secure position

and I do not have to return,
for here I have fulfilled the task
only for myself.

(The Climber)

There is a larger view as well, which makes the quest for poetry a vastly wider enterprise. This is reflected in a poem by Ivan Lalić, "The King and the Singer," which removes the smaller note of personality from the will to poetry:

And so in the end, your Excellency,
we are powerless, both of us:
From the wedding of this song
comes a heaven, a more dangerous earth,
and the multitudes we cannot control.

And every night
the familiar stars
slip further and further away.

The first poem speaks of obstacles created by man; the second deals with the nature of words and the nature of the universe.

The nature of the poetic word and the need to keep on uttering it are examined in many variations:

I search for my voice in the savage calm of the sea;
the sea turns to stone.
In the yellow desert of the autumn I search;
and the autumn grows green . . .

(Aco Sopov, *I Search for My Voice*)

You wait for a moment to adapt yourself to words
But there is no such poet
Nor a world fully free

O bitter and blind sea
In love with shipwreck.

(Branko Miljković, *Sea Without Poets*)

And in spite of the need to sing, great weariness comes from the burden of being a culture bearer, as in "Lament of a Stone" by Jure Kastelan:

Return me to rocks, to gorges, to mountain ranges
To the eternal laws of my virginity.
Hurl me into the sea, the oceans, deliver me to thunder.
Lords of the earth, give me peace and sleep.
Let not the hooves of your armies ring.
Nor tears flow.
Take me from the pavements, from the thresholds
    of prisons and cathedrals.
Let lightning and storms lash me. And stars
    crown me.
        And you, o hand holding a chisel,
Do not give me the life of a human . . .

And yet, Yugoslav poetry is full of energy, much of which is drawn from two great thematic strains. One is an insistence on reaching an all-encompassing knowing and the other is the recurring question, posed with quite some variety, "Great gods! What are we to do about our history?"

The knowledge toward which the poet strives is sometimes verbal, sometimes conceptual. There is a cumulative impression that this knowledge must be sought so intensely just now because there has been a great and disorienting rift in time. There is a time before and a time after. It is never hinted that "time before" might have been a Golden Age. Nor would it be admissible simply to call it the time before the Revolution of 1945. After all, much of the struggle between the poets and the politicians has been waged over the right to interiorize the Revolution rather than to apostrophize it. Time before is a period when man thought that the hierarchy of social and personal values was clearly defined and understood, even if without approval. Over and over, names and metaphors are borrowed from time before, in order to create some bridge of understanding now, in time after.

Knowledge and understanding are sought in words which are prayed for:

> My whole being begs you:
> Discover a word that resembles a simple tree
> And the palms of a hand, petrified and primevally naked,
> that is like the innocence of each first prayer.
> For such a word my being is begging you.
>
> (Aco Šopov, *The Prayer for Simple but not yet Discovered Word*)

There is an urge to understand human dynamics. Vasko Popa captures and imprisons hope, love, talent, inspiration and mystification in a little box and a white pebble. Then he can manipulate these human traits and observe them without being caught in the trap of old sentimentalities. The intensity with which he describes the use of the little box in his cycle "The Little Box" can perhaps be commented upon, but the sparsity and directness of the language causes the little poems to stand as definitions of all that is most important to a human being:

> Don't open the little box
> Heaven's hat will fall out
>
> Don't close her for any reason
> She'll bite the trouser leg of eternity
>
> Don't drop her on the earth
> The sun's eggs will break inside her
>
> Don't throw her in the air
> Earth's bones will break inside her
>
> Don't hold her in your hands
> The dough of the stars will go sour inside her

What are you doing for god's sake
Don't let her out of your sight

(The Craftsmen of the Little Box)

Another tactic used in the effort to order the universe is a ritualistic naming for salvation either of the namer or of the named. In "Cro-Magnon" by Gregor Strniša, a society survives by naming, but realizes by a powerful effort of the will that the names are not eternal:

Perhaps we have called these things
by their names;
those who come after us
will understand better . . .

. . . .

The heavy track of the beast is in the earth.
That one we'll never get to know.
Those who come after us
will find some name for her too.

But in "The Holy Mass For Relja Krilatica" by Milorad Pavić, it is the named one who is supposed to be saved, if he can survive the burden his name puts on him:

Rejoice you who sleep with a finger in your ear
Good tidings will come to you
For you are the one who ties a knot in his own moustache
So not to forget your name . . .

. . . .

You'll tie another knot one name in each moustache
Neither Relja to the Serbs nor Hariton to the Greeks.

The urge to grasp and to set up usable correspondences is so strong in this poetry that several themes which are of major importance in older poetry here lose their independence. One such theme is Nature. Classically, we expect to find a poetry of nature which celebrates process—the juggernaut of germination, ripening and death with rebirth. And we expect a poetry of man in nature, either acquiescing or rebelling but conscious of the moment in which he is confronted. The case is quite different in the poetry we are considering here. Blaže Koneski has written a poem about autumn and a tree whose leaves are falling, "The Tree Trunk." Here, nature functions only as a glass through which to see:

The fallen leaves are calling
those few leaves which still,
afraid of the uncertainty of falling
tremble upon the tree:
'Come down and die with us,
escape the high winds
into silence, close to the ground.
Strip bare this burnt out skeleton.
Make him stretch his black arms into space;
Let his body sink to the bed of the river,
below the waters of the autumn rain,
and we shall crowd thickly around him,
so he can never step out
from the circle of his yellow memories.

Is this an exercise in letting human feelings vibrate in tune to Nature, or a game of letting Nature reflect, for a moment, the emotion of a man? This would be an incomplete reading. Besides partaking of the old tradition of Nature poetry, these lines express the hostility of the ruled against the ruler, the hatred of the many against the monolith which holds them together. They announce that if the only way to evade the pressure of power is to die, then that might be a possibility to consider. Certainly the lines establish a sense of polarization which is a frequent image in this poetry, now drawing a line between civilized man and barbarian, now between words and deeds and always asking: Is there also a line between good and evil?

I have lived between my two hands
as between two brigands,
neither of them knew
what the other was doing.
The left hand was foolish because of its heart,
the right hand was clever because of its skill,
one took, the other lost,

they hid from each other
and only half finished everything.

Today as I ran from death
and fell and rose and fell
and crawled among thorns and rocks
my hands were equally bloody.
I spread them like the cruciform branches
of the great temple candlestick,
that bear witness with equal ardour.
Faith and unfaith burned with a single flame,
ascending hotly on high.

(Edvard Kocbek, *Hands*)

The position of nature in the poetry of this collection is that of a tool, a
library of images and metaphors. It seldom appears as a powerfully
functioning entity which man can observe although he is a part of it.
Nature has become strange and man must find another source of wisdom:

the landscape has lain down
behind its image.

. . . .

I cannot recollect
a formula to set me free.

(Edvard Kocbek, *Landscape*)

But man still has enough memory of what nature used to mean to him to
be able to recognize disorder and even be stimulated by it:

Over all maps the birds do not stir. Men struggle through
fantastic landscapes. Warfare of dogs and moonlight. Mad trees

have made a circle with silence and all is now a faultless
mummy. If only this instant would come to its end,

I too would start to call myself a mummy. But the gods
are kind. When we give them human power they keep quiet.

With us, though, things are different. Sometimes the truth
of black things descends on me and I wish to burn once again.

(Bozidar Timotijević, *The Truth of Black Things*)

And this disorder can be read as being many things: the fever dreams of the
poet's fertile sensibilities, or a derangement of the world that man has
made. Process now is not in nature, it is in man. It is travel, the birth of a
song, the formation of a human reaction.

Another large theme which is at its most characteristic for Yugoslav
poetry when it is subordinated to something else is that of love of one
human being for another. There are, of course, lyrics celebrating dedica-
tion, passion, a woman's body, but the love poetry which is the strongest
and most complex is that where images of love and images of knowing are
intertwined. One of the most striking of these is "The Living River" by
Borislav Radović. Here, a dark love brings a primal knowledge, important beyond words:

You tease, I accept. I make you a sister, dark and humble,
submissive. The returning skies are dark above us.
The image cannot be dissolved. Your braided constellations seek me out and give me direction; the strokes
grow lighter. Instead of any effort I leave my blackness within you. Here we are a single wound, a single
blade.

A lighter variation of this theme is found in poems which compare the
ways in which men and women love. In Milivoj Slaviček's poem, a man
gains knowledge from love:

In the end you will be only a poem
and a memory when I am ill: in darkness, half an hour
                                before midnight
when the city roars outside in the fog
You will be a small friendship with the World

You will give a needed charm to this or that facade
                                        once and somewhere
to this or that place deserted without traces
in the shadow of a journey when a good and quiet
                            sea plays on the walls
in a shadowy afternoon: I tell you, everything else is in vain.

(A Little Poem About Love)

In Slavko Mihalić's poem, on the other hand, a man tries (in vain?) to impart knowledge with love:

Look at those clouds, Vera, why are you silent
For God's sake, I am not a beast, but here is the rain
How suddenly it turned cold
We are far from the city

All right, Vera, I'll never forget your presents
We are now one, and why speak . . .
. . . .
Of course this place will remain sacred in my memory
Please hurry and don't turn back.

(The Approaching of the Storm)

As the rage for knowledge subsumes themes of love and nature, sometimes using them as comforters, sometimes as antagonists, an awareness grows that we have here a poetry of dichotomy. This is the way that a good many poets have chosen to cut into the existential mass and now, it is the plane upon which they must observe it: I looked for you and I found busy ants; are you Relja or Hariton?; I do not want the river, I want my bank; are we gay or are we sad. . . . It is in this alignment of the universe on two opposing sides that the poetry makes its most profound political statement. It divides the world into "we" and "they" but largely avoids definitive labels, thus intimating that the game is in the search rather than in the finding. Perhaps even more significant is the ruthlessness with which the sphere of political competence is widened to embrace all human activity; politics becomes a matter of all of life, and there is no little closed circle where it is acceptable to be part of "they" rather than of "we."

There are very few openly political poems in this collection. The most overt one is "Merrymaking," Milivoj Slaviček's little compliment to the TV programmers, and a standard piece of satire:

The eighth lecture about mental hygiene and the fifteenth
                    about abundant moral deviations
Then again popular music
Contemporary language in life and literature
Then again popular music
The history of my people and its cultural heritage
Then again popular music and cheap movies

One might even think we were very gay.

Much more characteristic for Yugoslav political comment is the poem "At
Last It Is Time For Man To Happen," also by Slaviček:

At last it is time for man to happen
(And man is not custom but wish, he is not a director
                                                but a friend)
for his desire and spirit to happen
for his Exit to happen: his brotherhood and activity
it is time for love to happen
for the Journey to happen
for essence to happen . . .

The yearning for some sharp, discontinuous experience of ecstasy to lift
man out of safe grayness is found more than once in Yugoslav poetry, but
the really significant spark in this poem is the word "director." Only a
socialist poet could include such a flatfooted word in a poem meant to be
exalted; the existence of a privileged director class is an inescapable reality
of socialist existence. But only a Yugoslav socialist would dare to make so
strong an attack on this class as to equate a director with a non-man.

The second great theme in Yugoslav poetry is history—not so much
memory or the power of the past over the present but graphic details taken
from the past of the nations of Yugoslavia and usually presented as a
problem of choice. Sometimes, history is present in a poem to set the scene
and to contrast the pastoral beginnings with the interests of the present.
Then it is often intertwined with folklore. But the poems in this volume
reveal, in their translated state, very little influence of the Yugoslav
folklore. This is because where the oral literature has been an inspiration, it

has largely made itself felt in the prosody of the poems and in minute allusions: here a horseman, there a deserted courtyard. Occasionally a poet will write a piece which contains a refrain reminiscent of Serbian oral poetry, and this is still visible in translation. But on the whole, it must be concluded that it was the poets, and not the poems themselves, who were nourished by the ancient oral tradition.

When the poets reach for a time and a way of life remote from their own, they are far more likely to look at their early recorded history, and the time most often tapped is the period of choice between high civilization to the East or West and near-barbarous pioneering. Ivan Lalić considers this difference in "Byzantium II," with an eye to the problem of human needs, and finds the choice not simple:

> . . . . The struggle goes on:
>
> To bear the loneliness,
> To bear this exchange of splendor
> for barbarity and to gain nothing—
> not even freshness—in return,
> to bear without relief
> the weight of this heavy solemn
> sentence . . . .
>
> . . . .
> The Almighty One in the gold luxury
> of his dome, in the magnificence
> of his pure absence
> repeats a gesture or true benediction . . .

Ivan Slamnig, on the other hand, pictures the Slav as an interloper in a Roman settlement—a committed barbarian:

> His eyes are wild, his coat is the yellow lynx;
> Now as I look at him he moves
> Away from the column and along the horizon . . .
>
> . . . .
> See how tall he is, how beautiful;
> See how wild he is, ah how wild he is . . . .
>
> . . . .
> What did he come for, Drusus,

With sheaf and bow
In his coat of fur?

. . . .

He came to pinch a god of our house
Just for the fun of it,
He came to rob us
To beat us to death
And not to give a damn.

(Siesta at Naronna)

The tensions within these poems and between them reflect an irony, sometimes shimmering and sometimes cutting, which is the enlivening spirit of Yugoslav poetry. How deeply sophisticated Lalić's Serb must be to call himself a barbarian after meditating on Byzantium and then rejecting its form of life. Or did he accept it upon becoming an Orthodox Christian? And how brave Slamnig's Croat, who knows that he can only dare to call himself a culture bearer if he will first admit that he arrived as a barbarian.

The poetry of the immediate postwar era, when it can be seen as a whole, is stern, forceful, and often cerebral behind its cloak of forests, water, and dark fires. Perhaps its ambitions and dissatisfactions can best be seen in this poem by Jovan Hristić, addressed "To Phaedrus," who yearned for the sublime:

This too I want you to know, my dear Phaedrus, we lived
In hopeless times. From tragedy
We made comedy, from comedy tragedy.

But the important: seriousness, measure, wise exaltedness
And exalted wisdom, always escaped us. We were
On no one's land, neither ours alone,

Nor someone else's; always a few steps removed
From what we are, from what we ought to be.

O my dear Phaedrus, while you stroll
With virtuous souls on the island of the blessed,
Recall at times our name:

Let its sound spread in the resonant air
Let it rise toward this heaven it could never reach
So that at least in your conversation our souls find rest.

On Translation

Throughout their cultural history, the South Slavs have been copious translators, at first out of hunger and then out of intelligent curiosity. Now, by a nice swing of the literary pendulum, the nations who have translated so much are themselves being translated, also out of curiosity and hunger. This new direction is fruitful because we want and need it to be. But just what is the fruit?

The feasibility of translating a poem from one language to another depends very much on how the poem functions. If its import is carried largely by the meanings of words or the contrast between meanings, it will be possible to translate the poem without an overwhelming sense of dilution and incompleteness. But as soon as the style of the language is made to be part of the meaning of the poem, the translator is in danger of producing an English version so stripped of its original force that it is little better than a retelling. This would be the case when a poem is built on dialect, puns, word play, etymologies, or tight rhymes. One would, for instance, hesitate to translate a tightly rhymed poem like this:

Kad frulaši tužne pospe
Zaključavši svoja čula

Po gluvoj se zemlji prospe
devičanski cvrkut frula.

U ožarju mlade sete
Pretvorene u golube

Zlatokrile frule lete
Nad ustima što ih ljube.

Style that adds signification to a poem is not always an insuperable hindrance to the translator. This is especially true when an effect is achieved through a strong contrast in the level of style—a leap from a declamatory tone to the speech of everyday life. There is, for example, a poem by Bogomil Gjuzel about Dojčin, a Macedonian epic hero, which uses such a leap to great effect:

DOJČIN'S AGONY

Savage is the law decreeing you be born alone
And alone fashion the doom that brings destruction.
But yet more dreadful is to be confounded
By the snare of unborn fruit.
If mother and country were not damned by us,
They would return our malediction twofold.

And so I lie in a tower of air
Thick-swaddled in folds of mist and snow,
Expecting the day that fate has promised
When I will unlock the world with a new damnation
And tense for the last blow.
I waited for the light that would save me,
Tunneled through the night of my parents.

I stepped on wonderworking springs and grasses,
Fouled my weapons with smears of blood,
And again I lie in pain in the White City, the bitter city,
And again, nothing is going to happen . . .

The last line is the only one which contains neither an inversion nor a great, heavily-loaded word. The flat finality of the very ordinary last line is something that can be transmitted in English.

It is more difficult to deal with the frequently encountered device of inserting a public, political cant word into an otherwise lyrical text. But words such as "director" or "primitive means of investigation" do not creep into the poetry by accident or through incompetence. They are used for their shock value within the texture of the poem and also as a forceful source of irony. It would be a mistake for the translator to smooth such words away with circumlocutions, and they must be understood by the foreign reader for what they are, and not as mistakes.

There are many losses occurring in translation which are due to the nature of the original language. In the present anthology, however, we are always dealing with translation from one Indo-European language to another, and both languages allow for the same logical and many of the same grammatical functions. Therefore, the losses with which we are concerned are almost never absolute losses of meaning. What the poem suffers in translation is an impoverishment of nuances, intensity, devices. It is a truism to weep for the assonances, alliteration, and rhyme that are lost, or even for the loss of the vowel quantity and pitch which are characteristic of Serbo-Croatian and contribute to the nature of its prosody. But it *is* of interest to see what is lost along with these ornaments.

Slavic languages offer a means other than rhyme for creating patterns that join words without the help of syntax. This means is based on the fact that large families of words may be built on the same root so that, for instance, a poem could be shot through with this thread: *dar* (gift), *darivati* (to reward), *darovit* (talented), *dariv* (given, though unearned), *darenik* (one who receives a gift), *darežljiv* (generous), *udar* (a blow). In a poem, a chain of words built upon the same root is seldom as long as this, but even a two-word series can have a strong effect. The following examples, though seemingly trivial, are offered because of their clarity:

KIŠA PRIČA I PRIČA: TO JE PRIČA STARA
the rain recounts and recounts: that is story old

OSTRVA LEBDE PRED NAMA, ZALIVI SE OTVARAJU I ZATVARAJU
islands float before us, bays open and close

OSTAJE POSLEDNJI ZIMSKI SAN KAO PRIČA VEĆ ISPRIČANA
remains last winter dream like tale already told [completely]

PO KROVOVIMA, VANI, DIMNJACI BEZ DIMA
on roofs outside chimneys without smoke

The languages of Yugoslavia impart a sense of economy: there are no articles, except in Macedonian; many pronoun subjects can be omitted because they are implicit in the verb ending; because of the tendency to word building, many diminutives, pejoratives, and indications of verbal time can be expressed in single words. Many highly specific nouns and verbs must be translated into two or three words in English, and as a result, the translation may sound wordy, tentative, less direct than the original. Finally, what is lost is the sound of a frequently onomatopoeic language, delivered in a sharp patter without diphthongs or nasals. Only very rarely, by great skill and greater luck, can this sound be approximated in English. This list of perishables in the original poems does not represent an argument that a classically wrought poem, existing in an aura of strict meter and rhyme, should not be translated. The following sonnet by Skender Kulenović remains a fine sonnet in English. And yet it must be confessed that the music of the original is gone.

Stećak mramorni ćuti govorom scena na boku.
Jači od kandža kiše, povampirenja i kradje.
Njegov mjesec i sunce, što znače posmrtne ladje.
Davno su prevezli dušu, vjekuju sad u doku.

Udaljili su se od njega gradovi i sela.
Vidik mu stvore listopad i koze što tu brste.
Vjetar podsjeti lijeske, i one se šaptom krste.
Zmija mu krene uz reljef, svoj reljef svije sred čela.

Zašto sam došao ovdje kad sve već ovdje piše?
Poslednju blijedu zelen s jesenjom travom dišem
Čuj, zvoni zrelo stablo: to lijes mi teše žuna.

Stihove što još bruje—dlijetom po stećku svom stišaj
i, uspokojen, pusti nek ih pokrije lišaj,
lezi pod stećak stiha bez prevoznika-čuna.

THE STELE
The marble shaft is still and eloquent with carvings,
Stronger than the talons of the rain, a vampire's bite or looting.
Its moon and sun, conveyance for the dead,
Have borne the soul away and lie eternal at the dock.

Cities and towns have moved away from it,
Leaf-fall and cropping goats make up its view,
Wind prods the hazel bush to cross itself and whisper,
A snake glides over the relief, its own relief a coil on the shaft's brow.

Why have I come here, if all is written here already?
I breathe the last green paleness in the autumn grass,
And hear a mellow trunk ring as a bird pecks out my coffin.

Silence the verses that still hum, your chisel on the shaft,
And softly let the lichens cover them.
Lie beneath the marker of your lines, without a funeral barge.

What is left when everything that must be surrendered in translation has
been stripped away? A structure of ideas, themes, images, contrasts—
almost, one would say, the sketch for a poem. But sometimes, what we
have is still a poem. The fact that so much of the contemporary poetry of
Yugoslavia can be successfully translated reveals much about the nature of
this poetry. Its essence does not lie chiefly in melody or linguistic device.
The old, secure rhythms learned from Western European poetry are being
replaced by new ones, which are often achieved by repetitions similar to
those of tone row music. A resavoring of the physical and moral essence of
small human actions provides a melody. The excitement which once
sparked out of a poem where matter and manner coincided perfectly now
emanates almost entirely from deeper within the poem. The element of
the poem which it is essential to transfer from one language to the other is
the manner in which the poet frames a little segment of life, the way in
which he confronts the physical with the spiritual. Even when the poet
moves away from actuality to allegorize self-knowledge into games with
stones, like Vasko Popa, he is not working his mysteries so much with the
surfaces of words but with cores of meaning. Indeed, one of the great
poetic preoccupations in Yugoslavia today is the search for changes and
constancies in meaning after the events of the past thirty years.

In spite of difficulties, much has been preserved and transmitted in the
poems of this volume. However, the English poems are not objects of the
same category as the originals. They demand to be experienced in a more
cerebral way. Explanations ranging from word histories to national history are needed to intensify understanding to the level the poet was
reckoning with. Perhaps some of the immediacy and wholeness of poetry
could be restored to a translation if it were received not with more
explanations but at the same time as some non-verbal event—music,
pictures, rhythms. The sense that possible delight lies in this direction is
born of the intuition that before a text can truly be shared from one culture

to another, it is not only the poem but also the reader that must be translated.

Gertrud Graubart Champe
Augustana College
Rock Island, Illinois

CONTENTS

xliv   •

Contemporary Yugoslav Poetry

TRANSLATORS

Elliot Anderson
Gertrud Graubart Champe
Howard Erskine-Hill
Bogomil Gjuzel
Anselm Hollo
Jovan Hristić
Bernard Johnson
Ahmed Muhamed Imamović
Branka Imamović
Carolyn Kizer
Alasdair MacKinnon
Mirko Magarasević
Maria Malby
Vasa D. Mihailovich
Ronald Moran
A. R. Mortimer
Aleksandar Nejgebauer
Joachim Neugroschel
Anne Pennington
Graham Reid
Tomaž Šalamun
Michael Scammell
Charles Simic
Biljana Šljivić-Šimšić
Veno Taufer
C. W. Truesdale
Celia Williams
Charles David Wright
Matthew Zion
Rudolf Zrimc

DESANKA MAKSIMOVIĆ 1898–

Born in Rabrovica near Valjevo, Desanka Maksimović studied in Belgrade and Paris. She taught school for many years, and has spent most of her life in Belgrade, where she lives and writes poetry.

Maksimović began to publish poetry after World War I. In the period between the two wars she wrote poetry and literature for children. After World War II she wrote several poems in which she expressed concern for her suffering people, along with hatred for the former occupiers of her country. In the last few years she has written perhaps her best poetry, evoking the glory of the Serbian distant past, while searching in it for illumination of the present. Her best postwar books of poetry are: *Pesnik i zavičaj* (Poet and His Native Land, 1946), *Miris zemlje* (The Scent of the Earth, 1955), *Tražim pomilovanje* (I Seek Mercy, 1964), and *Nemam više vremena* (I Have No More Time, 1973).

Her poems are distinguished by strong lyricism, genuine emotion, an almost pantheistic closeness to nature, simplicity and immediacy, and refreshing image and metaphor. These characteristics have remained constant throughout her creative life.

FOR ALL MARY MAGDALENES

I seek mercy
for the women stoned
and their accomplice—the darkness of the night,
for the scent of clover and the branches
on which they fell intoxicated
like quails and woodcocks,
for their scorned lives,
for their love torments
unrelieved by compassion.

I seek mercy
for the moonlight and for the rubies
of their skin,
for the moonlight's dusk,
for the showers of their undone hair,
for the handful of silvery branches,
for their loves naked
and damned—
for all Mary Magdalenes.

Mihailovich

FOR LIES SPOKEN OUT OF KINDNESS

I seek mercy
for those who lack the courage
to tell the evil one that he is evil
or the bad one that he is bad,
for those who hesitate
to hurt with the truth,
for the people who lie out of kindness.
For the man who would rather be humiliated
than humiliate,
for the man who has no heart
to pull down a mask when he sees it
on someone's face,
for people who cannot insult
those of different thoughts and creeds,
for those who never could
pronounce a sentence to others,
for whom all judges seem strict,
for every kind untruthful story
and other similar weaknesses.

Mihailovich

FOR ACORN

Shipbuilders are building ships for you,
Falconers raise falcons,
bees bring you honeycomb from the sun,
Fishermen fish for gold in the sand,
Peasants harvest fruits in the fields,
Hunters gather stag horns,
Monks copy for you gospels,
Painters present you with icons and frescoes,
Blacksmiths forge monastery gates,
juniper trees pour incense into censers,
Jewelers carve golden icon lights—
but I beg you for acorns,
acorns under the forest branches,
for a hungry child to rejoice
when he finds them in wintertime.

Mihailovich

THE SNOW ON THE GRAVE

The first snow on your grave—
one more icy barrier
between your nights
and my days.

The first snow on your grave—
not even a foot high,
not even the height of a hand,
but it seems
a glacier has descended upon your face,
a hundred tons of snow
have fallen between you and me,
between your silence
and the echoing of the bells.

The snow has once again locked
the door behind you;
it has fallen on you heavier than all the weight
of the earth and stones,
and its whiteness
has hidden you from me this morning
more cruelly than darkness.

Mihailovich

NOW IT IS CERTAIN

Through the same gate I shall enter too.
The shadow will rush toward me
as one always rushes to a newcomer
arriving from the region
from which we were banished.

Their faces will be both different
and the same,
as every night the face of the moon
is different and the same again.

But I shall recognize your faces
were they woven of darkness
or shining with an inner glow;
they'll give themselves away by a small sign,
perhaps by a smile they had on the earth,
perhaps by the familiar sorrow in the eyes,
perhaps by the arch of the eyebrow.

Mihailovich

EDVARD KOCBEK 1904–

Edvard Kocbek was born in Videm na Sčavnici, Slovenia. He studied at several universities, became a professor and later participated as a Partisan in World War II. After the war he was active for a while in political life but later turned exclusively to writing. His collections of poetry are *Zemlja* (Earth, 1934), *Groza* (Terror, 1963), and *Poročilo* (Report, 1969). He has also written memoirs and a book of short stories.

Kocbek has written sparingly, but his poems reveal a completely contemporary spirit, which makes him closer to the young poets like Šalamun, than to the older figures like Bor. His well-crafted poems, quiet in tone, cast an ironic eye on the world; not the irony of a man who feels superior to what he sees, but rather that of a man who is an endless victim, who is inevitably tied to what he abhors. His vision makes no allowance for romantic consolations, containing the hardness and convictions of a man who has deeply experienced life.

HANDS

I have lived between my two hands
as between two brigands,
neither of them knew
what the other was doing.
The left hand was foolish because of its heart,
the right hand was clever because of its skill,
one took, the other lost,
they hid from each other
and only half-finished everything.

Today as I ran from death
and fell and rose and fell
and crawled among thorns and rocks
my hands were equally bloody.

I spread them like the cruciform branches
of the great temple candlestick,
that bear witness with equal ardor.
Faith and unfaith burned with a single flame,
ascending hotly on high.

Taufer & Scammell

LANDSCAPE

The scent of wild animals
nears the houses,
pregnant women's
lips move,
ripe space smells
of oily stuff
and darkened corn.
Fruit has fed the worms,
roses have returned
to the nocturnal beehive,
the landscape has lain down
behind its image.
The silence rattles anciently,
memory weighs anchor,
moonlight plays
with a peacock's tail.
Things grow bigger
from their presence,
drunkards cannot drink enough thirst,
animals cannot reach the bottom
of their innocence,
the wind feeds on precipices
and darkness on thieves.
The world is riddled
with homesick pains,

I turned in a charmed circle
as in wedding dreams,
I cannot recollect
a formula to set me free.

Taufer & Scammell

A LONGING FOR JAIL

I was too late for the most important
spiritual exercises of my life,
I am left without a proof
of my true value.
Each jail is a treasury,
a secret drawer, a jealous
torture chamber, the most important stage
of a butcher's martyrdom before he is
corrupted by a naked woman holding a knife.
I missed the delight of that love,
I would die easier if I had counted out
the squares on the floor of my solitary
and completed in my thoughts the transparent frescoes
on the dusty pane
and gazed through the walls
at the frontier posts of mankind.
Now you have collapsed, my cell,
disintegrated to openness,
the world no longer consists of redeeming cruelty,
it is but a sabbath courtyard.
You can test me no more,
I am no longer a figure for the Christian crib,
for a puppet show or display of robots.
I am preparing myself for a different game—
look, I am turning into a little grey mouse,
my hiding places are all around,

tonight I shall sleep in the sleeve of a child
with no right hand, tomorrow I shall dream
in the echo of a shadow that sleeps after its voyage
through a fairytale that has no end.

Taufer & Scammell

THE STICK

What shall I do with my stick
now that it has begun to outdistance me?
Shall I throw it on the fire of a shepherd,
or give to the lame man on the road,
or to scouts reconnoitering the promised land?
Or shall I raise it in the air
to still the people's tumult,
or use it to trip my brother
so he breaks his leg in the dark?
Or shall I throw it into the sea
to save a drowning man,
or plant it in a field
to stand in the wind as a scarecrow?
Or shall I hang it in a pilgrim church
to increase the number of relics,
or bury it in a wood
so the bailiffs can't find it?
Or shall I give it to an ignorant father
so he can use it to tame his son,
or leave it out in the dew
so it turns green again?
Or shall I hand it to a choirmaster
to harmonize the voices,
or give it to an eager boy
to use it to prop up his tent?
Or shall I divine a spring with it
in order to water the desert,

or use it to conjure bread
from a stage magician's hat?
No, I will do nothing of the sort,
for all that is risky and foolish—
I will break it over my knee
and throw it down a deep ravine,
so that its heavy notches
may measure my fall.

Taufer & Scammell

DIALECTICS

The builder demolishes houses,
the doctor advances death
and the chief of the fire brigade
is the arsonists' secret leader,
clever dialectics say so
and the Bible says something similar:
he who is highest shall be lowest
and he who is last shall be first.

There's a loaded rifle at the neighbor's
a microphone under the bed
and the daughter is an informer.
The neighbor goes down with a stroke,
the microphone's current fails,
and the daughter goes to confession.
Everyone clings to a ram's belly
when sneaking from the cyclops' cave.

I hear in the night discordant music
coming from the circus tent,
sleepwalkers walk the highwire,
wobbling with uncertain arms,
and their freinds yell underneath
to rouse them from sleep,
for whoever is up must come down
and whoever's asleep, let him sleep more soundly.

Taufer & Scammell

MAK DIZDAR 1917–71

Mak Dizdar, a Croatian poet, was born in Stolac, Herzegovina. He went to high school in Sarajevo and later devoted his life to literature and journalism. He edited many newspapers and journals and spent the last years of his life as a free-lance writer. He was also a life-long student of the ancient and medieval literature of Bosnia and Herzegovina.

His books of poetry include *Vidovopoljska noć* (Night at Vidovopolje, 1936), *Plivačica* (A Swimmer, 1954), *Povratak* (Return, 1956), *Okrutnosti kruga* (The Cruelty of the Circle, 1960), *Koljena za Madonu* (Knees for the Madonna, 1962), *Minijature* (Miniatures, 1965), *Kameni spavač* (Stone Sleeper, 1966), and *Pjesme* (Poems, 1968).

Dizdar's poetry is characterized by a strong evocation of the past, expressed in a very personal and vigorous style. In his best book, *Kameni spavač,* he searches for the meaning of the inscriptions on the ancient tombstones, *stećci;* in reality, searching for his own roots. Much of the spirit of the old literature of Bosnia and Herzegovina is reflected in the dominant tones of his poetry.

THE BLUE RIVER

No one knows where it is
We know little but it is known

Behind the mountain behind the valley
Behind seven behind eight

And even farther and even worse
Over the bitter over the torturous

Over the hawthorne over the copse
Over the summer heat over the oppression

Beyond foreboding beyond doubt
Behind nine behind ten

And even deeper and even stronger
Through silence through darkness

Where the roosters do not sing
Where the sound of horn is not heard

And even worse and even madder
Beyond sense beyond God

There is one blue river
It is wide it is deep

A hundred years wide
A thousand years deep

About the length do not even think
Jetsam and flotsam unmending

There is one blue river

There is one blue river
We must cross the river.

Mihailovich

A COMPASS

Above is the polar star
and below Venus
here the northern Wind
there the Southern
who will tell me where
the path of love is
where
the path of death.

Mihailovich

VERTICAL AND HORIZONTAL

How shall we bury the screams deep into the ground of forgetfulness
So not to catch up with us on these painful journeys
How shall we gather all dear words and smiles into these tight wallets
How shall we shoe these wounded feet with a tough leather
Let sadness and all its companions stay behind us
And let the bones of the useless dead sparkle deeper and deeper
Instead of the procession torches
In this dark dough
Of the unknown.

Mihailovich

GORČIN

Here lies
The soldier Gorčin
In his land
Inherited by
A stranger

I lived
And called for death
Night and day

I did not step on an ant
Went into
The army

I was
In five and five wars
Without a shield or armor
So that one day
Suffering
Would cease

I perished with a strange illness

It was not a spear that pierced me
It was not an arrow that shot through me
It was not a sabre that cut me

I perished with an incurable
Illness

I was in love
But they took my girl
Into slavery

If you meet Kosara
On Lord's
Roads

I beg you
Tell her
Of my
Faithfulness.

Mihailovich

THE SEVENTH DAY
THE BOOK OF GENESIS
Chapter one

. . . And I saw the water eating away the earth
The sun drinking the water
The earth belching out fire
I saw beast attacking beast
Man spilling man's blood
I saw evil deeds on all sides
I saw the evil deeds thou didst create
For I had tasted of the fruit of the tree of knowledge
I saw for my eyes were opened
And I cried out
It is not good   It is not good   It is not
This thy earth
Is good only for the stones . . . .

Pennington

JURE KAŠTELAN 1919–

Born in 1919 in Zakučac near Omiš, Croatia, Jure Kaštelan studied at the University of Zagreb and obtained a doctorate in Slavistics. He participated in the war as a Partisan and later worked in various capacities in the cultural field, until he became a professor of Yugoslav literature at the University of Zagreb. He has also been a lecturer of Serbo-Croatian at the Sorbonne.

Kaštelan has written poetry, short stories, drama, and academic literary studies. He also translates from several languages. He began to publish poetry in 1940—*Crveni konj* (A Red Horse), and his later collections include: *Pijetao na krovu* (A Rooster on the Roof, 1950), *Biti ili ne* (To Be or Not, 1955), *Malo kamena i puno snova* (A Few Stones and Plenty of Dreams, 1957), *Čudo i smrt* (Miracle and Death, 1964), and *Izbor pjesama* (Selected Poems, 1964).

Kaštelan's early poems deal largely with his war experiences, stressing the pathos of sacrifice and suffering. In his more recent poems he is searching for a modern expression, striving to be more personal and sophisticated. At the same time, he is melancholic and even pessimistic; the horrors of war being replaced by the anxiety of modern man. Kaštelan is considered one of the best of the contemporary Croatian poets.

LULLABY OF KNIVES

Go and do not turn back. You lead the dead in a column.
Sight your gun at first violets. Sleep in your boots.

> Dark knives
> seek your throat.

Do not drink from the wells, they are poisoned.
Mountains have croaked from the snakebites.

        Dark knives
        seek your eyes.

No dream in which lovers sleep restlessly,
or the echo which lingers in empty gorges and ravines.

        Dark knives
        seek your heart.

Dark knives rattle your lullaby.
        The dawn you see faintly is cut
        into two equal halves
        of dream and blood.

Simic

LAMENT OF A STONE

Return me to rocks, to gorges, to mountain ranges,
To the eternal laws of my virginity.
Hurl me into the sea, the oceans, deliver me to thunder.
Lords of the earth, give me peace and sleep.
Let not the hooves of your armies ring.
Nor tears flow.
Take me from the pavements, from the thresholds
    of prisons and cathedrals.
Let lightning and storms lash me. And stars
    crown me.
            And you, o hand holding a chisel,
Do not give me the life of a human.
Do not give me a heart, reason, nor eyes
    to look with.

Back to the marbled seas, to dreams and mists return me.
Lords of the earth, give me peace and sleep.
     And you, o hand lifting the chisel, do not wake me.
Do not give me eyes to look on crime.

Mihailovich

A FORTRESS WHICH SURRENDERS NOT

I am a forest with only one flag—the heart.
Invisible walls built out of wounds.
I resist invasions
with a lullaby.
I am transformed in an armor of dreams.
Sentries keep watch on all towers, and on the shore
reeds and tamarisk hide the little boats.
Weather-vanes look upon the distant iron armies
as they sharpen their arrows,
grease their muscles and thighs and prance
on wicked steeds of tin and fire.
The bridges have been lifted. Mighty currents
guard the gates.
The moon disappears at dawn and the bright sun emerges.
I am a fortress with only one flag—the heart.
I am a fortress which surrenders not.
The dead, freed of their senses, do not surrender.
Lightnings, in their swift flight, do not surrender.
The living, with gem-like eyes, do not surrender.
Strongholds surrender, but not those made of dreams.
These give up and defend themselves alone.
I am a fortress with only one flag—the heart.

Malby

INTO DARKNESS

Into darkness, into the night
of blood, of flesh
for the imperial crown
dead bodies decay
on the highway
a soldier student
in the ancestor's mud
wounded limps
down the borderland
down the waters
and iron bird
flew into the sky.

Mihailovich & Moran

ACO ŠOPOV 1923–

Aco Šopov was born in 1923 in Štip, southeastern
Macedonia. He participated in the war as a Partisan and afterward studied at the University of
Skopje. He has served as an editor of many periodicals and in publishing houses. He is currently a
director of the publishing house *Koɕo Racin*.

His first book of verse, *Pesni* (Poems), appeared
in 1944 as the first collection of poems in contemporary Macedonian poetry. He has published several additional books of poetry: *Pruga na mladosta*
(The Railroad of Youth, 1946), *Na Gramos* (To
Gramos, 1950), *So naši raci* (With Our Hands,
1950), *Stihovi za makata i radosta* (Verses of Sorrow
and Joy, 1952), *Slej se so tišinata* (Merge with Silence, 1955), *Vetrot nosi ubavo vreme* (The Wind
Brings Nice Weather, 1957), *Nebidnina* (Fate,
1963), and *Gledaɕ vo pepelto* (A Gazer into the
Ashes, 1970). Šopov is also a translator.

Together with Koneski and Janevski, Šopov is
one of the founders of contemporary Macedonian
poetry. A subtle lyricist, a sensitive observer, and
a poet of intense personal experiences, he has enriched Macedonian poetry at the very beginning of
the new period, thus creating models for the
younger poets. He was also one of the first to
liberate Macedonian poetry from a prevalent
non-esthetic criteria in the late nineteen forties.

I SEARCH FOR MY VOICE

I search for my voice in the savage calm of the sea;
the sea turns to stone.
In the yellow desert of the Autumn I search;
and the Autumn grows green.
My arms are not my arms

(my arms with fingers of moonlight).
My eyes are not my eyes
(my eyes, eyes for a distant sight).
From the hard jaw of the time my word proceeds
and springs up in the fields with the teeth of seeds.

Gjuzel & Erskine-Hill

THE PRAYER FOR A SIMPLE
BUT NOT YET DISCOVERED WORD

My whole being begs you:
Discover a word that resembles a simple tree
and the palms of the hand, petrified and primevally naked,
that is like the innocence of each first prayer.
For such a word my being is begging you.

My whole being begs you:
Discover a word from which—as soon as uttered with a cry—
the blood begins to ache insanely,
blood that seeks a channel to flow.
For such a word my being is begging you.

Discover such a true word
resembling those peaceful prisoners
and that wind, that spring wind,
that wakes the fawn in our eyes.
Discover such a true word.

Discover a word about birth, about wailing,
discover such a word. And this temple,
enveloped in its antiquity and huge from waiting,
will open by itself obediently.
Discover a word about birth, about wailing.

Mihailovich

THE HUNT ON THE LAKE

A poised bird. Full of greed.
An upright threatening cormorant.
The lake surface calms down
blue from all the wept out sorrow.

A dark blow of a wing
darkly cuts the blue of the water,
soaring up into the cold air
a fish torn apart in its beak.

The day is grey from dying.
We are alone, without words.
Some mute understanding
forces us to part ways.

Mihailovich

POEM

Be the earth unyielding and hard.
Be a mute statue on the table.
Mock the flight of time. And ugly,
grow out of the stone of sorrow.

Be the sky. Be my blueness; A sheaf of stars.
A living time between four walls.
Pierce deep into the heart. Like a spear.
And support me like a caryatid.

Mihailovich

from FATE

I have traveled long, traveled all eternity
from myself to your fate.
Through flames I have traveled, through ruins,
through ashes.
In scorching heat, droughts, on forbidden roads.
I have eaten the bread of your beauty,
drunk from the throat of your song.

Do not look at these black dry valleys
slitting my face—
the face of the earth gave them to me.
Do not look at these uneven marks on my back—
the fatigue of the hills brought them to me.
Look at these hands—
two fires,
two rivers
of dark waiting.
Look at these palms—
two fields,
two droughts
of deaf wailing.

I have traveled long, traveled all eternity
from myself to your fate.

Mihailovich

SLAVKO JANEVSKI 1920–

Slavko Janevski was born in 1920 in Skopje and began to write poetry during World War II. He published his first collection, *Krvava niza* (A Bloody Garland), in 1945, one of the first books in contemporary Macedonian poetry. Since then he has published several more collections: *Pruga na mladosta (The Railroad of Youth, 1946)*, *Pesni* (Poems, 1948), *Egejska barutna bajka* (The Aegean Gunpowder Fairy Tale, 1950), *Lirika* (Lyrics, 1951), *Leb i kamen* (Bread and Stone, 1956), and *Evangelie po Itar Pejo* (Gospel According to Itar Pejo, 1966). He also writes short stories, novels, travelogues, film scenarios, essays on literature and the visual arts, and literature for children. His novel *Selo za sedumte jaseni* (A Village Behind Seven Ash Trees, 1952, 1965), is considered to be the first Macedonian novel.

Not only one of the founders of modern Macedonian poetry, Janevski continues to be one of its leading poets. His poetry, whether about his war experience or about his intimate concerns, is characterized by a picturesque quality, originality, boldness, and even a touch of black humor. In form, he is just as bold, imaginative, and innovative.

SILENCE

When the poppies pull themselves up from their roots
and start out
one after the other
toward the sunset,
do not follow them.
There are no weddings any more
and at each step stands autumn
ridiculous, white and bare.

When the poppies leave behind them devastation,

shut up the rain inside you.
Let it ring in the gutter of your veins
beneath a familiar ceiling.

And be quiet.

When the wind falls upon your window
with three thin cries
and the weeping of a half-grown crane,
again be quiet.
The poppies hate speaking.

Gjuzel & Erskine-Hill

THE POEM OF A SOLDIER
SIX FEET UNDER THE GROUND

I am no more.
The sinews of my throat
remained on the bellflowers.
In the twilight the winds
lie on them.
    Good night, birds.

I am no more.
The darkness of my eyes
remained on dark blue waters.
In the twilight the whirlpools
drink them thirstily.
    Good night, fogs.

I am no more.
The fingers of my hands
remained under the grass.
In the twilight girls gather
flowers.
    Good night, nights.

I am no more, no more.

The sinews vibrate in pain:
"Olive-tree, support the sky
not to tumble down."
The eyes burst from water:
"Let branches sprout from us,
we come from your seed."
The fingers beg the grass:
"Wrap us in your bark, tree,
the frost is hurting us."

I am no more . . . .

On my forehead lies
a good night
a heavy night
a long night.

Mihailovich

A GIFT

The night is the laughter of all men . . .
This night, my night, good night,
this night the streets are white ambushes
in their thirst for light
in their hunger for laughter.

But I have two hands. Look:
in the one I carry bread and wine,
in the other a secret.
Let us drink this night; be a tide,
quiver like leaves,
murmur like waters,
be soft like the sky.
Friends: this hand is yours.

This night, this long night,
I stand like a tree trunk
having only one hand left
but even a hundred would be too few,
for I was thirsty
for I was hungry
for I was alive.

This night, girls, this night
in this hand is my secret
about a reed tall as the proud crown of the head
about clouds white as breasts
about the sun melted on someone's lips,
this night, girls, surely this night,
this hand is for one of you—
for a secret more secretive than all secrets
for a reed more slender than all reeds
for a cloud . . .
For a burning heat on someone's lips.

Mihailovich

THE SONG OF THE ETERNAL SAILOR

I left along the distant roads, my apple tree, and now you bloom alone,
my heart is my helmsman, blind yet seeking blue bays,
if I hear the wind in the evening, I forbode your ruin . . .
Has someone's hunger pulled you out by the roots
as I roamed alone?

When the blackbird whistles shrilly three times at dawn,
do not wait for the sun. Listen, I am still digging roads,
on a mast I carry a black flag from tavern to tavern
and hide the pain under my skull.
Oh does the blue lightning bring you a blue downfall
and do the rains lash you?

I have no more strength to come calm and tall
and to lean my forehead against the sleepy water,
from the blows to rest my hands on the rye until dawn,
and then to go nowhere . . .
My apple tree, the autumn is already here, there is no shore to sail to.
And so I dream of a secluded, small, and deserted harbor.

Mihailovich

ZVONIMIR GOLOB 1927–

Born in Koprivnica, Croatia, Zvonimir Golob studied at the University of Zagreb. After a short service as a librarian, he became a professional writer. He has been active in many cultural projects—served in various capacities with periodicals and publishing houses, translated prolifically, and has edited books by domestic and foreign authors.

His books of poetry are: *Okovane oči* (Chained Eyes, 1946), *Nema sna* (No Dream, 1952), *Glas koji odjekuje hodnicima* (A Voice Echoing in Halls, 1957), and *Elegije* (Elegies, 1963).

Golob employs his own peculiar approach to surrealism, but is also concerned with existentialist as well as social problems. His love poems, perhaps his best work, are emotionally charged and suffused with passion.

ASHES OF FORMER THINGS

I was and remained what I was
accidental foam
knot that bends
seen from a distance
crooked sun but sweetest of all
under the noble salt
heart that must be lost
but now it's already here
near the flesh.
I was and remained what I was
only memory
between two waters
only fire
closed in a glass
that you can't see through
if such fire can exist
or such glass.

This is not warmth that repeats itself
nor fire that can be preserved
it's not a plant
or an animal
nor a thing—
a crack in which we store
cracks of tears
closed seed.

I bent myself in the joints of flowers
grown to the sky
with teeth hard with fear
I broke the wings of butterflies
and closed their eyes
arranged into tiny mounds
kindness
and confidence
lit and again lit the light
in a lizard's nest covered with stamen
and now all that
truly tiring
rips confidence bit by bit
into the common cause
of the heart.

He who stood alone
on one side
and threw bits of glass
in the bucket hidden far under the earth
into the root of hearing
with a hand untouched by rain
he who opened the doors and he
who forgot how they open
he who planted and again planted
the seed of madness
in his own blood
threw the grain of the wind
to the four cardinal points

and listened to the sound of his steps
on the surface of the well
like a wet herd of bees
that caress with poisonous love.

He who listened how the hoar frost burns
and kept in the other hand
the skill of death
strength to forget
strength that brims over
only a single step
a single step beyond himself
or next to himself

he who forgot how to forgive
or taught how to forget
he who looked into the light
and lost his sight
he who dreamed reality
and in reality dreamed
it doesn't matter
he who imagined love
and gave her shape
he who imagined the years
and added death at the end
like a tall marble wall
beyond which there's nothing
and before which there was nothing
only ashes
only ashes of former things
too much to be nothing
too little to be everything
or almost everything

he who gave and took away and he
from whom they took and gave nothing in return
each united in the fire of his own childhood
will become water that falls far from the tree

will become rock
and will float on the water
like burning oil
like rock that burns
like water that burns
like water that burns
and turns into ashes
under the smoking stars.

The night closes itself
bitter surface of incense
ashes of former things
settling on the palm from which we drink
on lips through which we drink
on the body
open to the water that decomposes
in tiny fences of the heart,

space most of all.

I was and remained what I was
a crack
in which we store
cracks of tears
black face of the snow
closed seed

with its space and its fence at the end.

Simic

THE BODY OF A WOMAN

> *Cuerpo de mujer, blancas colinas,*
> *musclos blancos . . .*
>
> *Pablo Neruda*

The body of a woman, a hidden miracle unknown in you,
is there a tenderness greater than mine
while you sleep graceful, in the shadow of your radiance?

Diving into you as if into an underground river
I repeat the names of flowers in order to explain you:
petunia, azalea, robinia hispida.

While you sleep you are playing, your river into which I dip
my hands, saddened and eternal
with your pebbles of mother-of-pearl and burned moss.

On you I recognize everything and marvel at everything:
there in the abyss from which I came and to which I return,
and a salty thirst comes to me as you are dying, o sweet suffering.

Look how much I seek you: as an echo its voice,
as a voice its echo that does not cease
and burns in my blood, in my head without light.

Look how much I desire you: as an empty water surface
its whirlpool to agitate and exhaust it there
where everything begins, and from where death does not move.

Is there anything more beautiful than your metal,
than your fruit offering itself? I am a ship
sinking and swaying between your shores.

There you are, conquered and naked, but who will pass
under the arch of triumph with the wreath of bitter laurel?
In your dream I too am lost forever.

Staring at limitless space I open
part after part of your body that differs no more
from me within me, equal and equally alone.

There is an invisible song too that transforms
all your miracles into one, trembling in the rain,
and the accursed sky that wounds, cries behind your eyebrows.

Mihailovich & Moran

ANATOMY ATLAS

I want to see the body of a black man on the fifth page of Anatomy:
sinews
his heart,
precious blood
closing in the bloodstream of joined veins,
arms that bore the cross
and three times stumbled with it,
eye that watched the bewildered fire of the south,
fingers that counted the dead and fists that broke the chains,
kidneys that pissed blood on the pillar of shame,
neck that hung from an oak tree
for that reason planted
in hot fissures of the earth
like a black flag raised at half-mast
on the feast-day of madness,
ear-drums pierced by curses,
limbs carved,
violated,
beaten
on crossroads that lead
to four sides of despair.

I want to see the body of a black man,
black body
where the anchor of a whip left its sulphurous stamp,

on the fifth or seventeenth or no matter which page of Anatomy,
so I can say: this too is my body
as loud in its hour of death
as humiliated in its love;
a sob shakes it
restless and naked in its innards,
a sob, constant sob, proud and powerless
like the muffled sound of a pulse in the throat of condemned animal,
black face of conscience imprinted in color
on finest paper
so that I can see the forehead, spat on, despised,
so I can measure the warmth of flesh, depth of suffering,
strength of hate and love,
and all that can't be measured,
weighed,
reached,
all that separates us and brings us together
in common human brotherhood,
so I can understand
find out
at last
why my eyes and my blood
my skin nourished in a glass tube between electrodes
and adding machines
between concrete pillars and pus-oozing synthetics
should be more worthy than his skin
fertilized by sunlight.

Simic

A SIMPLE DEATH

I

Created from and for a dream
you stop me
before the doors of a simple death
and I change

into a bird
and a river
backing up to its source.
Your name, that voice resembling silver
left in the throats of bright quails,
that is the night opening the eyes
of an eternal butterfly
and fires of sure springs.

III

You are a fire in which fingers tremble,
a knife cold and sharp in the moon's groin,
a word which is not and death:
a sad game we have not yet learned.

I think no longer of the desperate grass,
and the cries of the stones of terrible kisses,
once again I fear that the doors may be closed
to thousands of horses afraid of dreams.

All who are forgotten in the darkness
seek their hands in the womb of the hyenas
and only one handsome shepherd
will find the flock of lost ants.

A woman cries in the corner.
Who will cover her mouth with earth?
Who will close the eyes of cautious shells
with the hand of glass, sand, and pine cones?

Mihailovich & Moran

SO FALLS THE AX

They say that the cold is coming,
emptiness and loneliness, the wind arrives visiting
the double forest, and the dense rain

touches with its cold tongue
the forehead of the earth. Be here, beside me,
like my hand, open to receive with you
what awaits me. To give and to take,
the same word into which love enters
like into bed.
To whom does a man belong if not to you, tenderness,
to whom love if not to those
who build a stake at which the heart of the earth still burns.
As if I were not born, as if I had died already
hidden in a rose, in a dream somebody else dreams,
in the fever of the plants, in the water or the air
which you will inhale before you depart.
They say that the cold is coming,
but the fate of all is only my fate,
and the pain of all does not become greater. Death for all
is only death for me and therefore I want to be
so that everything I see can exist:
ants with their examples which I fear,
the tolling, the bread, the scent of a woman,
the naked fruit without consequences, some knowledge,
misfortune, pain or a sound of a trumpet in the mud,
so that the world can exist, history or a kiss
and finally you, my love, my hoarse bell,
my territory fenced in by wire
to which the wave of the sky climbs.
They say the cold is coming, the time of emptiness,
but I expect nothing because what is coming
I already possess struggling, in order to fall one day
more quiet than when I spoke
the words which only you did not hear.
So the tree of the woodcutter tumbles.
So falls the ax!
So does the snow I am expecting.

Mihailovich

VESNA PARUN 1922–

Vesna Parun was born in Zlarin near Šibenik, Croatia. She studied at the University of Zagreb and has been a free-lance writer ever since. With her first poems, written in a modernistic manner, she contributed substantially to the struggle against the conservative forces in literature.

She has been writing poetry and poems for children since 1945. She has published more than twenty collections of poems, including: *Zore i vihori* (Dawns and Whirlwinds, 1947), *Crna maslina* (Black Olive, 1955), *Bila sam dječak* (I Was a Boy, 1962), *Vjetar Trakije* (The Wind of Thrace, 1964), and *Ukleti dažd* (Accursed Rain, 1969). She also writes plays, critical essays, and translates Bulgarian poetry.

Of Croatian woman poets now living, Parun is undoubtedly the best. Her idiom is one of intimacy and confession in content and pure lyricism and femininity in tone. She blends her emotionality with a thoughtful approach to the basic problems of human existence: love, especially of women; closeness to nature; and death. Her poetry appeals to both the senses and the mind. Above all, her easy flowing, melodious verse, makes her one of the best contemporary Yugoslav poets.

AN INVITATION TO SILENCE

My arms are a hut of reeds in the middle of a swift water.
All around darkness and night. The clouds are stalking the earth.

Will you approach me among leaves in quiet gardens
in a dream to heave my white meadows, my white flax?

The forest is calming down, the wind is calming down,
                    the road has withered,
The mountain is alone. No one is coming. The yellow moon

squats on the shore, the entire long evening waits on the shore.
And the river is dark, the river is deep, the river flows on.

Mihailovich

A RETURN TO THE TREE OF TIME

You who ask where I find the courage
to sing like a sun about love again
once I had locked it in a chest of black song
and laid it into a bird's lap.

Listen: I always return to myself
and a discovery waits for me in the bark of each tree
that I cut with the knife of memory.

But if the tree has died
and has nearly become coal,
I will plunge my hands deeply into the soil
and will dig it out as a coal.

If I return in ten years
I will dig it out as a stone.
But if I return in a hundred or more years
I will dig even deeper, and will find nothing.

For, even a stone does not remain a stone.
For, even a stone also migrates somewhere.
Do not ask about its journey
but let me sing and return
to the root of my song, the deepest to me.

Mihailovich & Moran

YOU WITH HANDS MORE INNOCENT THAN MINE

You with hands more innocent than mine
and with the wisdom of nonchalance,
You who can read his loneliness
from his forehead better than I,
and remove the slow shadows of hesitation
from his face,
as the spring wind removes
the shadows of clouds floating above the hill

If your embrace gives courage to the heart
and your thighs detain the pain,
if your name gives rest
to his thoughts, and your neck
is a shade to his resting place,
and if the night of your voice is
a grove still untouched by storms

Then stay by him,
and be more devout than those
who had loved him before you.
Beware the din that approaches
the innocent nests of love.
Be gentle to his sleep
below the invisible mountain
at the edge of the roaring sea.

Walk along his shore.
May the saddened dolphins meet you.
Wander in his woods. Friendly lizards
will not harm you.
And the thirsty serpents that I tamed
will be humble before you.

May the birds which I warmed
in the nights of sharp frost sing to you.

May the boy who on a deserted road
I protected from spies caress you.
May the flowers I watered with my tears
bring fragrance to you.
I was not blessed to witness
the best years of his manliness.
I did not receive his fertility
into my bosom ravaged by glances
of cattle drovers at fairs,
and those of greedy thieves.

His children
I shall never lead by the hand. And the stories
which I prepared for them a long time ago
maybe I shall tell weeping
to poor little bears
abandoned in a black forest.

You with hands more innocent than mine
Be gentle to his sleep
which is still innocent.
Yet permit me to see his face
when years unknown to me
begin to descend upon it.

And tell me at times a thing or two about him
that I may not have to question wondering
strangers and neighbors
who have pity for my patience.

You with hands more innocent than mine
stay by his headrest,
and be gentle to his sleep!

Malby

THE HOLIDAY OF BLINDNESS

If we had true eyes, if we were not born blind,
We would see around us neither landscape nor orchards.
We would see how an old city grows old, how a wind dies.
We would see how the rules of the game reverse,
How essence touches essence, thought motion.
We would see a man asleep on the palm of a large plant
That carries him through the night and disentangles
   his shadow.
We would see ourselves not surrounded by others: cut
By their short path through our transparent flesh.
We would see ourselves in a mirror already grown
   with our kernel into others.
As we watch a storm, so we would watch upright
The touching drama of mutuality, ourselves mixed into it.
If the old belfries of noon had eyes, how ashamed
This non-existing I of ours would be
And how it would fall on its knees.

Mihailovich & Moran

IF ONE COULD GO AWAY

If one could go away, if one could mount a horse
and go forever, or beguile an old ship
into taking us out of the city,
a friend would leave a friend, a mother would abandon children.
Houses would crack from tears of those who remain,
mountains would turn green from the song of those who are leaving.

But I do not know with whom I would want to await the dawn:
with those who cry or with those who sing.
For those who cry will slowly console themselves
and those who sing will tire of their song.

I would never leave on a horse or on a ship
because all those I want near are already far away,
because I have no one to flee from. And because I am afraid of returning.

But if one could leave forever, and truly leave with a song,
I think I would take a long leave from those places where I wept,
never forgetting those who were at least once happy
because of me and who, smiling, forgave me.

Mihailovich & Moran

A HOUSE ON THE ROAD

I lay in the dust by the road
neither did I see his face
nor did he see mine.

The stars descended and the air was blue.
Neither did I see his hands
nor did he see mine.

The east turned green like a lemon.
Because of a bird I opened my eyes.
Then I recognized whom I have loved
all my life.
Then he realized whose poor hands
he has hugged.

And the man took his bundle and set out
crying for his home.
And his home is the dust on the road,
just as mine.

Mihailovich & Moran

BLAŽE KONESKI 1921–

Born in 1921 in Nebregovo near Prilep, Macedonia, Blaže Koneski studied at the universities of Belgrade and Sofia. Since 1946 he has been teaching the history of the Macedonian language at the University of Skopje, where he is the dean of liberal arts. Koneski was instrumental in laying the foundation of the scientific work on the Macedonian language, and was the author of its dictionary. He has also written a number of scholarly works on linguistics, philology, literary history, and is a prolific translator.

His first book of poems, *Mostot* (Bridge) appeared in 1945. His other collections are: *Zemjata i ljubovta* (Earth and Love, 1948), *Pesni* (Poems, 1953), *Vezilka* (A Knitting Girl, 1955, 1961), and *Reki* (Rivers, 1968).

Koneski belongs to the first generation in postwar Macedonian poetry and is one of its founders. His poetry is direct, intimate, and meditative. Macedonian motifs—mythical, folkloric, or contemporary—are frequently found in his somewhat traditional and subdued poems. Koneski is a master of controlled pathos and understatement. Above all, he has done pioneering work in establishing the right of Macedonian poetry to exist.

THE TREE TRUNK

The fallen leaves are calling
those few leaves which still,
afraid of the uncertainty of falling,
tremble upon the tree:
"Come down and die with us,
escape the high winds
into silence, close to the ground.
Strip bare this burnt out skeleton.
Make him stretch his black arms into space;
let his body sink to the bed of the river,

below the waters of the autumn rain,
and we shall crowd thickly around him,
so he can never step out
from the circle of his yellow memories."

Gjuzel & Erskine-Hill

VIJ

In my consiousness as in a midnight church
I locked you. And just as candles fade
when extinguished, so you grow pale,
and all the saints give you the eye.
Here you are a prisoner for whose sake
I have made many a powerful incantation,
and here already that hour has arrived
when all signs point to my appearance.
I come like that terrible Vij
eyes grey, the whole of me a thirsty earth,
yes terrible and the tenderness I bear
in hard clumps makes you pale.
I approach now as tender Vij but already
you have drawn the mysterious line
and soon as I move near that soil, abruptly,
the void collapses rock crushes rock.
And I, the all thirsty sand start crumbling,
burying all, impotent to rise again.
I, Vij, conjured you powerfully
but famished have no strength to reach you.

Nejgebauer & Zion

A CHILD SLEEPING BY THE LAKE

You are sleeping, little boy,
and the lake is absorbed in thought—
the lake is shaping your fate.
You are sleeping and it
creeps into your soul by the barely audible lapping of waves,
as into a bay with white pebbles,
in which every pebble can be descried.
You are sleeping,
but even its smallest ripple
leads like a thread to those loud waves
that will suddenly come to life, start crying and carry you on.
Sleep, little child,
the lake is shaping your soul
and awakening thoughts about your future days.

Mihailovich

THE WHEAT

Bold erectness of the girls
who are not afraid of their breasts.
Dark blue flowers are in their hair,
arms firmly pressed to the body,
but the fingers in thoughts thirstily extended
for the first touch.
Ah, that is the girls' choir—
leaning over the border of the stage,
we are waiting for it to hug us like a sweet wave,
but instead we are engulfed in the sounds of a powerful song
that enraptures and then immediately saddens us.

Mihailovich

DOJČIN'S AGONY

A mocking shadow spied out my footsteps,
Snake in a grave, slithered into my mind,
Cursed my laughter, stained my sorrow black.
I looked around mistrustfully, thought, meditated.
Then I felt laughable, infinitesimal and lowly.
My body melted
My hands hung boneless
My sword fell
And I fell down in pain . . .

. . . I thirst for the gloom of a frigid grave—
There is no end for me without my destined feat.

Unknown woman, alone on earth,
Sister and mother mine, you who have suffered much,
You who felt pain enough to make you stone,
Come, golden sister!
Gather up my moldering bones without terror,
Rebuild me,
Wrap me in three hundred ells of linen,
Speak the quiet word to me,
Set me upright.
Teach me to walk again, mother.

Put a sword in my hand—
To kill the black Arab—
To die.

Champe

STEVAN RAIČKOVIĆ 1928–

Stevan Raičković was born in Neresnica, Serbia, finished high school in Subotica, and studied literature at the University of Belgrade. He has worked in various institutions and publishing houses, and is now an editor for the leading Belgrade publisher Prosveta.

Raičković has published several collections of poetry as well as books for children. Representing the neo-romantic current in contemporary Serbian poetry, he employs several basic motifs: nature as perfection, passion for loneliness, and yearning for soothing silence. His anxiety over man's lost ties with nature leads him sometimes to pessimism and retreat from urban life. Simplicity and sincerity are his other traits.

His major books of poetry are: *Pesma tišine* (The Song of Silence, 1952), *Kasno leto* (Late Summer, 1958), *Kamena uspavanka* (The Stony Lullaby, 1963), *Stihovi* (Verses, 1964), *Prolazi rekom ladja* (A Boat Sails Down the River, 1967), and *Zapisi o crnom Vladimiru* (Notes About Black Vladimir, 1971).

STONE LULLABY

Sleep wherever you happen to be,
All you kind, bitter, inspired ones,
You hands in the grass, lips in the shade,
You who are bleeding, you who are in love.

Heal into the blue dream of the stone,
You living, you tomorrow assassinated,
You dark waters under the white foam
And bridges stretched over emptiness.

Cease herb, do not wither,
Sleep marigolds as the stone sleeps,
Sleep all you sad, all you weary ones.

Last bird, turn toward me.
Softly say this name,
And turn to stone in the air.

Simic

PEOPLE WAKE UP WITHOUT WEAPONS

The people enter the houses. They open the memory box.
  Close their windows.
Then for a while
On the sly
Look between curtains at the asphalt into the swaying circle
Thrown by some lamp.
Beyond the river
The people enter into mud-huts,
Their backs bent a little.
They listen too,
Somewhere above the forehead,
Now only
A diminishing
Play of air and reed.
On the trampled grass
Between the settlement and the city whose names are riddles
Asked by someone,
The soldiers
Dark from a dream
Stack up sharp pyramids of rifles.
Then they enter into a tent, their heads bent as if bowing.
Otherwise,
Everywhere around
Birds turn into leaves.
Snakes quite successfully imitate the cracks on the bark.
Waters and fish pass by each other,
Each to its own dream.
The wind has spread its tired skin on the hill slope.
Its profile melts in the dark air.

Under the sky
Begins to unfold from the roots
An interrupted memory each on its own headrest.
Then slowly
The stars with a familiar sign announce a metamorphosis,
And invisibly,
Quietly exchange the roles backstage.
The leaves turn into birds,
The snakes and cracks stir each to its own flower,
Each flower to its own sun.
Now it is clear what is air
And what is not.
That already is a hill in its obvious certainty.
The wind has disengaged itself and crawls its first step,
Its uncertain millimeter.
Otherwise
Everywhere around
Under the tin roof,
Under the grass roof or swamp reeds that whistles,
Behind the transparent pane which is lit,
In the stony chest of walls, colored half from a dream
    and half from the whitewash,
The eyes of all the living open.
The little circles
Innocent again.
The moment is short and should be caught by the reins
    on the spot,
People are waking up without weapons.

Mihailovich & Simic

THE BLACK SERVANT OF BIRDS

Come to high grass and let flowers kiss your knees.
They kiss exquisitely, like the only woman.
There I am lying too, spending my summer as I know how.
The grass trampled down by me during the day

Recovers in the brief night
and the blades again rustle like a forest.
At dawn, near the bottom, ants begin to creep again.
Every morning is pleasant here as every evening.
The noon sun burns me and thirsty I drink.
Later the shadow lengthens and hides me quietly.
At dusk, I lie back waiting for the brook of stars.

I, naïve master and black servant of birds,
want and yet do not want to see someone passing by.
Perhaps the blades will not rise again
Under somebody else's footsteps.

Šljivíc-Šimšíc

A BIRD

A bird, tiny speck in the sky.
Timid fierce plummage,
The soul of the blue!
I am watching your song of an arrow.
How I wish I were a tree or a dried-out stump.
Fly down on this good body without fear!
I shall be quiet as a stone and shall not let out a breath.
On my head spend a peaceful day.

Mihailovich & Simic

SONG OF THE GRASS

The grasses have a single thought heavy as a stone.
They tell me: Who needs your song.
Lie down. Fold your hands, anywhere, under your head
And keep quiet. Keep quiet until you forget speech.
Silently watch the hill quite distant and blue,
Sunk in silence. Lift your eyes slowly from the hill

To the cloud, so restless and white, moving in the sky.
Look from the cloud into yourself. And stopped in yourself
Lie down. Quiet with your eyes turned within, under a
                    cloud by the hill.
Confused by the dark inside you, look and understand simply:
(Simply as the wind sways us accidentally.)
There are no clouds above the hill a little black because
                    of the dusk.
I lie in the tall grass and think indefinitely.
An ant on my knee is like a man on a hill.
Restless, the ant stands. I'm silent. And this is my song.
Sunk in thought, I lie in the grass. The grasses rustle
                    heavy as a stone.

Simic

GANE TODOROVSKI 1929–

Born in 1929 in Skopje, Gane Todorovski published his first poem toward the end of the 1940s. He has served with periodicals and publishing houses and is now the secretary of the Union of Macedonian Writers.

His books of verse include: *Vo utrinite* (In the Mornings, 1951), *Trevožni zvuci* (Disturbing Sounds, 1953), *Spokoen čekor* (A Peaceful Step, 1956), *Božilak* (Rainbow, 1960), *Mečti i horizonti* (Dreams and Horizons, 1964), and *Apoteoza na delnikot* (Apotheosis of a Workday, 1964). He also translates and writes literary criticism and history.

Todorovski is a member of the second generation in postwar Macedonian poetry. As a poet of peculiar sensitivity and strong linguistic ability, he has enriched the contemporary Macedonian language. With his controlled diction and pronounced expressiveness, he has contributed significantly to the development of Macedonian poetry from the 1950s to the present.

from CALM STEP

I

Over the grey, huddled contours of the suburbs,
the twilight sows its dark dust,
and like a messenger of the coming night
it arranges the evening scenery.

The fresh smell of night leans against the senses.

I believe he thought the night was a small square
mercilessly boxing in all the lonely people,
and so he went toward its threshold,
went through noisy evening buried deeply in himself.

I believe the lonely ones are tempted by night's depths.
It is their only harbor hidden from all eyes.
Often in it the last prayers to the day are whispered,
often in it the absence of people is revealed.

I also believe he thought the night was a quiet clearing
where weary men seek brief rest.

Mihailovich

SEVEN RETURNS TO THE MOTIF OF THE ASPEN

I

Green eyelids of sleeplessness.
Mute, green rustling.
She's the beauty of the field
dying for sleep in its midst.

II

Her waist is the green color of a butterfly
imprisoned forever in a high vertical.

III

Yearning for peace she shifts restlessly,
quivers erect, stares at the clouds,
watches the road, pines for the nomads
and shivers in midsummer sultriness.

IV

Sinful, too-sinful frigid woman who has conceived,
does she suffer with sleeplessness or tremble with fear?

V

Had I been her godfather I would have named her Restlessness,
Unrest-Restlessness, a dry field hillock.
If I were the evening wind, I would nibble at her quiver,
quiver, that sign of timid loneliness.

VI

She'll tell you herself how timid she is—
always moving: Morning. Noon. Evening.

VII

She envies the birds
for the nests they've built within her,
and their offspring for their sleep and rest;
The insomniac, the barren one, the green restless one.

Mihailovich

A NIGHT WITHOUT PUNCTUATION

Toward the shore we sail
We
lonely travelers

This flared-up weariness hurts
If we could only find the way
to be born again
and again
into the naked mornings

And our bare thoughts
tremble
restlessness scratches
the skin of the night
In the boat of hope
we sail
toward you
O dawn
rising above the eylids
grown heavy

And no one has the strength
even a grain of strength

to put at least a comma

And the periods we hate

Mihailovich

THE EVENING RUFFLED BY WIND

The afternoon is poor in colors.
The greyness—
that ugly, confining decor.
Wrapped in stupid uniformity
the street stretches sadly,
and you sense so to speak
that familiar
that feverish emptiness
that so often settles on the city.
And it is just fine that it came tonight
this crazed
this exuberant
wind born for pranks—
may its non-existing hands blossom
to find peace and rest
this vagabond that can
brighten our foreheads,
rub our eyes,
redden our cheeks,
so that we yearn and immerse
childishly
into all ruffles of this world—
for it is delightful indeed
to entangle someone's curls
just as it is to pass from an empty afternoon
into the evening ruffled by wind.

Mihailovich

MIODRAG PAVLOVIĆ 1928–

Miodrag Pavlović was born in Novi Sad in 1928. He finished medical school at the University of Belgrade and practiced medicine for several years. Later he turned to writing as his main vocation. Now he works as an editor in the publishing house Prosveta.

He has written poetry, plays, short stories, and essays of literary criticism. His first collection of poems, *87 pesama* (87 Poems) appeared in 1952. His other books of poetry are: *Stub sećanja* (The Pillar of Memory, 1953), *Oktave* (Octaves, 1957), *Mleko iskoni* (Primeval Milk, 1962), *Velika Skitija* (Great Wandering, 1969), *Nova Skitija* (New Wandering, 1970), *Hododarje* (Pilgrimage, 1970), and *Svetli i tamni praznici* (Bright and Dark Holidays, 1971).

For his prevalently contemplative poetry Pavlović found sources in Anglo-Saxon literature and in classical myths. Intellectual and neo-classical, he endeavors to overcome the romanticist, Bohemian tradition of over-emotionalism. In his latest poems he turns more and more toward Byzantium, ancient Slav, and old Serbian myths and legends, at the same time creating his own.

Pavlović has also written short stories, *Most bez obale* (The Bridge Without Shores, 1956), and plays collected in *Igre bezimenih* (The Dance of the Nameless, 1963), *Koraci u drugoj sobi* (Steps in the Other Room, 1958), and *Put u neizvesnost* (The Road to the Unknown, 1958). His collection of essays *Rokovi poezije* (The Terms of Poetry, 1958) shows him to be an erudite and demanding literary critic.

HUNTING

I took my brother hunting
in the woods at dawn,
we had fine steeds

flint arrows
and the forest was swarming with wild animals
My brother, a man of few words,
understood the language of the animals
the wolves spoke to us about fraternity
the wild boars had the voices of our ancestors
and the birds the voices of our sisters
poor spinsters never married never born
for days on end we never stopped hunting
we wanted to unharbor the true prey

Then we returned to the village
starving and empty-handed
even the servants made fun of us
the unfaithful wives we had left behind
had absconded with the jewelry
Even the monastery refused
to offer us beggars food or shelter.

Only our horses remained faithful
they carried us off into the distance
and the birds soared over our heads
thrusting aside the clouds.

Neugroschel

THE FOUNDLING

You found me lying on leaves,
bearing a secret name, perhaps a vegetal one,
and I can't say who I am:
half my name remained on my mother's breast
half on the chapped lip of the giant.

Perhaps I'm the *guzla* rejected by a singer in exile,
perhaps the fratricide escaping vengeance
or the prophet who leaves

his thoughts like cobwebs
on the branches of oak trees.

Carry me off, you merciful carters,
high up in the winds on the peaks of the forest
to cool my wounds;
or else sell me on the slopes of the sea,
sell me to other countries, to rich cities
where in the gardens of tender mothers
aging giants gaze at the ocean
but never want to trample my forehead
with harsh feet

I can no longer spend each night watching
in the foliage the dense glow of uncreated beings
who study my suffering
for the wisdom of non-birth.

Neugroschel

THE CHORUS OF DOGS IN KNOSSOS

They yapped, they yelped beneath the walls:
men like maddened dogs,
and our voices made us accomplices
of those who had disembarked.
In the chaos they forgot to close the chambers;
we hounded one another over the royal beds,
we licked the bull's horns,
while the snakes coiled around the bars on the gates.
We had nothing left to lose;
we looked forward to defeat
so as not to be devoured by our masters.
When the Dorians smashed down the gates
they saw one of us on the throne
and they stood there gaping.
His nose stuck out
and its shadow darkened their faces.

They looted and plundered, but gave us no meat:
we petitioned them for greater privileges,
but all we could get was the king's body, a turd.
Should we devour it?
Why not?
Hadn't we already mounted the throne!
His flesh was as leathery as a strap
and the liver was gristly.
Next they came carrying chains
and they kicked us out to bay at the moon.
But it was worse for the snakes;
they broiled them on skewers.

We had hoped for a better life
under the new masters.

Neugroschel

THE BLIND KING IN EXILE

I write to you from the capital of the world
Here I sit at the window, I, an imperial guest,
listening to the noise of the street beyond the walls,
the chitchat of the falconers at noon
the shouts from the galleys at the docks.

This morning I knelt down on marble
and tonight I will listen to the singing of repentance.
I dine with fragrant ladies
and thus I live, exiled, in the imperial city
yet close to the different parts of the world.

I could have seen fabulous things here
if they hadn't torn my eyes out in my country.
I have to go back there to look for my eyesight.
But if I'm blind how can I find my country?
I know only the roads

at the bottom of my memory,
marked out by long chants that lead me by the hand
like clouds from one shore to the next.

If the messengers put me on horseback
if the speedy couriers lead me away
who can say what throne they might make me mount?
How shall I rule an invisible empire?
I can only be a servant
a beggar before bolted doors;
my father who blinded me in this world
will heal me in the next.

To my son I leave battles,
the crown and double vision.
Let him strike foreigners harder with his scepter:
as for me, I'll go off quietly to look for my eyesight.

Neugroschel

DUŠAN: THE CONQUEROR IN CONSTANTINOPLE

On Sunday the gates of the Eastern city
were thrown open for me
by angels speaking Serbian.
I felt I knew the secret of the city
and I spoke Greek on the square,
but when the citizens heard me they shouted:
that's not our ruler
and locked themselves up in their towers.

Next I climbed upward towards the serene sky.
Clouds covered with greening woods
formed an arch above the Bosporus
and many marble stairways
let down to the foot of the sea.

That was how the capital came
into my hands without wrath
and the domes of Hagia Sophia
were apples I received as presents.

When lights were lit
I began to give orders:
send messengers to Nerodimle
Launch vessels against the Turks
and serve dinner in the halls.
My new minister then whispered to me
that I needn't bother too much with affairs of state.
Evidently I hadn't noticed
that I had died two hours by horseback from the city
but he added that I was still a welcome guest
that on the upper landings rooms were awaiting me
prepared for the night and for my visit in the hereafter.

Ever since, I've had an important position
in the death senate of Constantinople
it's no use looking for my tomb in Serbia
no use desiring a different glory for me.

Neugroschel

QUESTIONNAIRE OF SLEEPLESSNESS

Who rattles in the keyhole?
Who builds belfries under my window?
Who weeps over the sad fate of the hero?
Who lets the lambs out of the gate?
Who drives the dwarfs out to pasture?
Who threw King's dolls in the bushes?
Who gave the alarm-clock to the bat?
Answers:
Small night celebrates the great night.
Cold. The message in armour stumbled and fell.

Who will point the way for me tomorrow?
Who will cook my lunch and hand me a letter?
Who rings now above my bed
and calls for the doctor?
Or does he call for the pilgrims to witness?
Who lights the great fence of kindlings?
The dawn already wiggles under the pillow.
Who has sent the urgent message
that there should be suffering?
And why has that message been directed to me?

Simic

VOICE UNDER THE STONE

Once I was born a tough outlaw
to spend my life in ambush
counting coffers of gold,
heads of the hanged in the trees.

Another time, a poor man,
I became a sly servant.
On Sunday in the middle of the church,
I cut the King's throat
and threw his body over the ramparts.

In one life I was born a beast:
rage brimmed-over from within me
like holy scent from a Saint.
I slaughtered all husbands and flocks,
ripped open the innards of trees
so they wept like a bad year.

At the end of every tale,
they gave me the King's daughter in marriage,
and kingdoms
(somewhere I still reign).

Only when I was born with streams,
clear and in embrace with birds,
my thoughts perished.
Turned to stone I sunk in the earth's throat,
and was never born again.

Simic

VASKO POPA 1922–

A native of Vojvodina, Vasko Popa was born in Grebenci near Bela Crkva. He studied in Vienna, Bucharest, and at the University of Belgrade, where he graduated. He has been active for many years as an editor in the publishing house Nolit. His poems have been translated into almost every European language. In 1968 he received the National Austrian Prize for European Literature. He is considered one of the leading poets in world poetry and certainly one of the best poets in contemporary Serbian poetry.

Popa has published several collections of poetry: *Kora* (Crust, 1952), *Nepočin-polje* (Field of No Rest, 1956), *Sporedno nebo* (Secondary Şky, 1968), *Uspravna zemlja* (Upright Country, 1972), *Živo meso* (Raw Flesh, 1975), *Vučja so* (Wolf's Salt, 1975), and *Kuća nasred druma* (A House in the Middle of the Road, 1975).

His poetry exhibits an elemental simplicity; a predilection for concrete objects; curt, crisp versification; and, above all, the creation of new myths. Despite his apparent traditionalism and deceptive simplicity, everything about Popa is unconventional, almost revolutionary. Even his patriotic poetry is unlike any other. Concern for the universal and even metaphysical, and an attempt to pierce the crust of things, make his poetry laden with meaning and symbols exciting to read and hear. He likes to write poetry in cycles, several of which are completed while others are still in process. With each new cycle it becomes apparent that his entire opus partakes of one vast and original vision of man and universe on an almost epic scale.

Popa is also interested in folk literature, gathering and publishing unearthed folk songs and tales, especially those with mythological overtones.

WHITE PEBBLE

Without head without limbs
It appears
With mad pulse of chance
It moves
With shameless pace of time
It holds each thing
In its passionate inner embrace

White polished virgin corpse
Smiling with the eyebrow of the moon

Simic

HEART OF THE PEBBLE

They played with the pebble
Pebble like any pebble
Played with them as though it had no heart

They got mad at the pebble
Broke it in the grass
Startled they saw its heart

They opened the heart of the pebble
In the heart a snake
Sleeping spool without dreams

They roused the snake
The snake gushed upward
They ran far away

They looked from the distance
The snake coiled itself round the horizon
Like an egg it ate it

They came back to the place of the game
No trace of snake grass or pieces of pebble
No trace of anything in the circle

They looked at each other and grinned
They winked at each other

Simic

DREAM OF THE PEBBLE

A hand springs out of the earth
It throws the pebble in the air

Where is the pebble
It didn't return to earth
Nor did it climb to heaven

What happened to the pebble
Did the heights devour it
Did it change into bird

Here is the pebble
It remained stubborn in itself
Neither on earth nor in heaven

It listens to itself
Among the worlds a world

Simic

LOVE OF THE PEBBLE

It stares into the beautiful
Round blue-eyed
Featherbrained eternity

It has turned into
The white of her eye

She comprehends it
Her embrace has
The shape of its desire
Dumb and bottomless

All her shadows
It has captured in itself

Blindly in love
And no other beauty
Except the one it loves
And will kill it
It notices

Simic

SECRET OF THE PEBBLE

It filled itself with itself
Did it overeat its hard flesh
Is it ill

Ask it don't be afraid
It doesn't beg for bread

Turned to stone with a sweat cramp
Is the pebble pregnant
Will it give birth to stone
Or a beast or a streak of lightning

Go and ask as much as you want
Don't hope for an answer

Hope for a bump on the head
Or another nose another eye
Or who knows what

Simic

ADVENTURE OF THE PEBBLE

Fed up with the circle
The perfect circle around itself
It came to a stop

Its burden is heavy
The burden within
It dropped it

The stone is hard
The stone it's made of
It left it

So narrow where it lives
In its own body
It stepped out of it

It has hid from itself
Hid in its own shadow

Simic

TWO PEBBLES

They look stupidly
Two pebbles looking

Two sweets yesterday
On the tongue of eternity

Two stone tears today
On the eyelid of unknown

Two flies of sand tomorrow
In the ear of deafness
Two happy dimples tomorrow
In the cheek of daylight

Two victims two little jokes
Silly jokes without a joker

They look stupidly
With their cold asses they look
Speaking out of their bellies
Into the wind

Simic

THE LITTLE BOX

The little box gets her first teeth
And her little length
Little width little emptiness
And all the rest she has

The little box continues growing
The cupboard that she was inside
Is now inside her

And she grows bigger bigger bigger
Now the room is inside her
And the house and the city and the earth
And the world she was in before

The little box remembers her childhood
And by a great great longing
She becomes a little box again

Now in the little box
You have the whole world in miniature
You can easily put it in a pocket
Easily steal it easily lose it

Take care of the little box

Simic

THE CRAFTSMEN OF THE LITTLE BOX

Don't open the little box
Heaven's hat will fall out of her

Don't close her for any reason
She'll bite the trouser-leg of eternity

Don't drop her on the earth
The sun's eggs will break inside her

Don't throw her in the air
Earth's bones will break inside her

Don't hold her in your hands
The dough of the stars will go sour inside her

What are you doing for god's sake
Don't let her get out of your sight

Simic

THE TENANTS OF THE LITTLE BOX

Throw into the little box
A stone
You'll take out a bird

Throw in your shadow
You'll take out the shirt of happiness

Throw in your father's root
You'll take out the axle of the universe

The little box works for you

Throw into the little box
A mouse
You'll take out a shaking hill

Throw in your mother pearl
You'll take out the chalice of eternal life

Throw in your head
You'll take out two

The little box works for you

Simic

THE ENEMIES OF THE LITTLE BOX

Don't bow down before the little box
Which supposedly contains everything
Your star and all other stars

Empty yourself
In her emptiness

Take two nails out of her
And give them to the owners
To eat

Make a hole in her middle
And stick on your clapper

76 •

Fill her with blueprints
And the skin of her craftsmen
And trample on her with both feet

Tie her to the cat's tail
And chase the cat

Don't bow down to the little box
If you do
You'll never straighten yourself again

Simic

THE VICTIMS OF THE LITTLE BOX

Not even in a dream
Should you have anything to do
With the little box

If you saw her full of stars once
You'd wake up
Without heart or soul in your chest

If you slid your tongue
Into her keyhole once
You'd wake up with a hole in your forehead

If you ground her to bits once
Between your teeth
You'd get up with a square head

If you ever saw her empty
You'd wake up
With a belly full of mice and nails

If in a dream you had anything to do
With the little box
You'd be better off never waking up

Simic

THE JUDGES OF THE LITTLE BOX

to Karl Max Ostojić

Why do you stare at the little box
That in her emptiness
Holds the whole world

If the little box holds
The world in her emptiness
Then the anti-world
Holds the little box in its anti-hand

Who will bite off the anti-world's anti-hand
And on that hand
Five hundred anti-fingers

Do you believe
You'll bite it off
With your thirty-two teeth

Or are you waiting
For the little box
To fly into your mouth

Is this why you are staring

Simic

THE PRISONERS OF THE LITTLE BOX

Open little box

We kiss your bottom and cover
Keyhole and key

The entire world lies crumpled in you
It resembles everything
Except itself

Not even a clear-sky mother
Would recognize it any more

The rust will eat your key
Our world and us there inside
And finally you too

We kiss your four sides
And four corners
And twenty four nails
And anything else you have

Open little box

Simic

KAJETAN KOVIČ 1931–

Born in 1931 in Maribor, Slovenia, Kajetan Kovič graduated from the University of Ljubljana, and now works as an editor in a publishing house. He is also active as a translator of German, French, and Russian poetry. His books of poems are *Prezgodnji dan* (Too Early a Day, 1956), *Korenine vetra* (The Roots of Wind, 1961), *Improvizacije* (Improvisations, 1963), and *Ogenj-voda* (Firewater, 1965). He has also written two novels and poetry for children.

Together with other poets of his generation, Kovič has struck a new tone in contemporary Slovenian poetry, attempting to discover a modern style and employing radical experimentation. His expressionistic poems reveal the sensitive contemplativeness of an intellectual immersed in the discords and contradictions of modern life. At the same time he is attracted by the primitive life in its primeval purity.

THE SORCERER

I believed
you were the master of masters,
who had conjured the world out of nothing,
with power over suns and moons,
a poet among creators,
for a long time I served you,
obediently and faithfully,
now I have smashed your vessels,
you were a sorcerer
in a grown-ups' fairy tale,
you cooked false gold
like all the silverbakers and goldcooks before you.

I, your sorcerer's apprentice,
do not like fairy tales.

You had a bad effect on me.
My tongue is lame from silence.
But don't worry
it will speak again.
I will scrape off the decay
and cleanse the words.
Then you too will hear me.
My apprenticeship is over.

Taufer & Scammell

BLACK PRAYER

Come, black word,
last desperate passionate voice
on the tip of my conscience,
bashful and daring voice
of love and anger,
word pure as fire,
razor word,
listen,
they are sounding the charge.

I am alone
in a trench on the edge of night.
No more do I have my golden spear
or golden shield.
Armies are bearing down on me in hordes,
greedy and sullen.
That's why I call on you, word of despair,
and draw you from the scabbard,
my last blade,
that's why I kiss you,
black
naked
sword.

Black word,
we are taking arms against black gods.
I shall look calmly into their faces.
I shall leave you on their brow,
leave you there mute.
For I shall not speak again
of those who are worth no word,
either white
or black.

Taufer & Scammell

OUR FATHER

Our father, Great Machine,
that giveth and taketh away
color, form and name,

that delighteth in having us the same, same, same
as machines in thine own image,

that hath forbidden all thorny plants,
for thine own hands
were pricked by a thorn,

tell us

where now can grow
the acacia's grief?

Taufer & Scammell

THE HOUR OF CONSCIENCE

Well, now you know; that's how things are.
No need to throw yourself down on the ground
And bite the stones.
No need to roar
For you are not an animal,
And what's more, you can't work miracles.

You fought with the machines,
But not in reality.
In fact you love them.
They are no worse than horses,
Nor are they to be blamed.
They are quite innocent,
The others are to blame.

You are yourself to blame
You stood too long upon the lonely brink
You stood too long upon the lonely brink
The old days turned to air
And your pastures are empty for ever more.
Why should you call back
What cannot be recalled?
Scan with your radar,
Change your wavelength.

You are born into this world
You know more about rust than pollen.
The bees will take care of that.
You must see to the rust.
Will you let everything corrode?

You are not a monument;
You are a living ant
And you must carry your small log to the summit of the world.
You are of no importance,
The important thing is the log.

And perhaps: the anthill.

MacKinnon

THE BULL

A young red bull detaches himself from the herd.
He looks among the alders for an herb unknown to others.
He is enclosed by the white hoops of windflowers.
He lowers his head and licks the warm weeds.

A knotted tree stops him short by the river.
In a spasm of anger the russet neck tautens.
Tiny rags of leaves flutter in the thicket.
He digs his horns in the ground and takes the strain.

The tree crashes onto the grey surface of the water.
He stands before it like a fiery god.
He returns to the herd drunk with power and freedom.
Wine-red is the color of his broken horn.

Scammell

TONE PAVČEK 1928–

Born in 1928 in St. Jurij near Novo Mesto, Slovenia, Tone Pavček finished law school at the University of Ljubljana and later worked as a journalist. He writes poetry, especially for children, and translates Czech, Polish, and Russian poetry. He is also active in organizing theaters for children.

He has published several collections of verse: *Pesme štirih* (Poems of Four, 1953), *Sanje živijo dalje* (Dreams Live On, 1958), and *Ujeti ocean* (The Captive Ocean, 1964).

Pavček is a member of the second generation of Slovenian postwar poets. Like many other younger poets, he is striving to give expression to his complex inner life in a modern poetic idiom.

FEAR

O gaping emptiness of the falling tree trunk,
o shyness of fluttering birds, fugitives from the winter,
o wild feverish dying of a fallen stalk,
o death in a thousand faces
from the cradle to the grave,
mystery and threat,
warning and the final port with the lighthouse of silence,
do not churn the waves, do not push my boat
toward the cold light, into the shoreless port,
barren, unreal like the echoing of the end
in the deaf space of the sea without shores,
let the trees grow powerful and slender,
let the birds nest in their crowns
and grassy shoots bloom at their feet
with a thousand faces
of the morning always dewy and young,
so that I could watch,
so that I could watch long, endlessly long,

how it sways on them, as on a willow swing,
a tiny ant and nimble thought,
born for the journey
beyond the cradle and the grave!

Mihailovich & Wright

MERRYMAKING

Is the game the meaning
or the meaning the game?

We have flattened the grass
and trampled the roses
to build a playing field
for endless merrymaking.

The playing field grew
and a big tower on it
resembling an elephant with giant tusks.
Monkeys swayed from them
nibbling bananas
and throwing the peels at the esteemed ladies.
A trench was dug in the middle of the elephant,
a large tunnel for promenade
from one end to the other,
from paradise and back to it.
Serious people came
and wondered about the merrymaking
and stern ladies came
and wondered about the merrymaking
children stopped by
and enjoyed themselves
until they began
to sing in unison: Enough,
the elephant is tired of walking
and the monkeys are fed up with bananas,

and children were attracted elsewhere,
therefore the people demolished the playing field
and knocked down the tower
and began to look for a new place
and a new field
and a new elephant.
The former merrymaking, the former playing field
they erased immediately from memory,
just as those before them had erased
flowers and grass.

Mihailovich

I HAVE STOPPED WEEPING

I have stopped weeping:

out of unreal dreams, which in reality
fall into dust,
out of palms, rough and scratched as is the world,
which, small and large as is the world,
eagerly make now order, now disorder,
out of eyes which dream of blossoms but look on horror,
out of all sunken ships and birds which have flown away,
out of the cage of the body, out of the prison of space,
out of the cave of humiliation and bars and barbed wire,
out of the dark of nightmare, through the crust of the frost
at length must pierce
a root
which will become a hope,

a plant which, where today and tomorrow meet
beneath the triumphal arch of the young morning,
will, like the blossoming ivy, clothe the bridge to the shore
of the future
where we will be many and where once more,
only this time from happiness, we'll weep!

MacKinnon

CIRIL ZLOBEC 1925–

Ciril Zlobec was born in 1925 in Ponikve na Krasu, Slovenia. He studied Slavistics at the University of Ljubljana and has been active ever since in cultural affairs. He is the editor of the leading periodical *Sodobnost*. In addition to poetry, he writes prose and literary essays, and translates Italian and Serbian poetry.

He made his debut with three other poets, Tone Pavček, Janez Menart, and Kajetan Kovič, in a book of poems, *Pesme štirih* (Poems of Four, 1953). Since then he has published: *Pobeglo otroštvo* (The Escaped Childhood, 1957), *Ljubezen* (Love, 1958), *Najina oaza* (Our Oasis, 1964), and *Pesme jeze in ljubezni* (Poems of Anger and Love, 1968).

In his early poetry, Zlobec seems to be preoccupied with the loss of childhood, which he laments and for which he tries to find solace and love. In later poems he turns to wider problems of the world and its insensitivity and ugliness, protesting man's incapability to escape them. Zlobec attempts to reconcile his lyrical sensitivity with his concern for basically prosaic problems.

ALMOST A HYMN

You are still without comparison,
not bare but shamelessly naked,
to be compared only to yourself,
no longer beautiful as . . . but beauty itself,
no longer bright but brightness itself,
no longer seductive but seduction itself,
no longer alive but life itself,
a cry that deafens itself
and silence to which it harkens,
a glance that grows blind from looking at itself
and sees blind,
a fire that is wild to go out,

peace that wakes up storms,
a storm that brings peace,
love,
white in bed,
green in the grass,
blue in the sky above,
red in the dawn,
dark in the night,
love,
its own only comparison,
no longer like a tree but simply:
upright as love,
not like death but simply:
love, horizontal like love,
you—I—the two of us.

Mihailovich

ALMOST A VICTORY CELEBRATION

Every life is almost
a victory celebration
And so is mine.
Every new day I live through
imposes upon me
a battle
which brings me certain
victory,
and the days I leave behind me
among all the defeated armies
are the only harmless ones:
all those dead and lost
days of mine.
I add victory to victory
day to day
and day after day
from victory into victory

I grow into my last
day, which is already sharpening the knife
for the pain
of my only defeat.

Mihailovich

SOMETHING IS TERRIBLE, TO TELL THE TRUTH

Traveling from port to port,
the sea hardens the cruising sailors.
When a storm bars their way to destination,
they always clear a new one through the stubborn waves,
forget the destination
thinking only of the journey.
Only the unexpected calm of a port conquers them,
quiets down the winds in their tussled hair,
banishes the restlessness of the horizon from their eyes,
and the healthy salt from their sunburnt backs
washes away with the smell
of the port prostitutes.

We have sailed into the dreamed-of future.
There are no more roads. Only a net of streets.
And you always return along them, after you've gone away,
children laugh at you when you tell them
that from generation to generation, for a hundred thousand years
and more, you have sailed on a ship of hope and unrest
through the winds into the future,
which suddenly is a road to no one.

It is terrible, to tell the truth
that we have realized man's thousand-year old dream.

Mihailovich

EVENING

All ways are shortened now;
They end and they begin
at home.

The world is bounded now
By this small circle of light,
Created by
The lamplight's glow.

The bed is fragrant now
Like the green grass;
The wife is like the earth
Waiting for rain
To quench her thirst.

MacKinnon

MILIVOJ SLAVIČEK 1929–

Milivoj Slaviček was born in Čakovec, Medjumurje, and studied at the University of Zagreb. He now lives as a professional writer.

He has published several books of poetry since 1954: *Zaustavljena pregršt* (Halted Handful, 1954), *Daleka pokrajina* (A Distant Province, 1957), *Modro veče* (A Dark-Blue Evening, 1959), *Predak* (Ancestor, 1963), *Noćni autobus ili naredni dio cjeline* (The Night Bus or the Next Part of the Whole, 1964), *Izmedju* (Between, 1965), *Soneti, pjesme o ljubavi i ostale pjesme* (Sonnets, Poems of Love and Other Poems, 1967), *Purpurna pepeljara, naime to i to* (A Purple Ashtray, Namely This and That, 1969), and *Poglavlje* (Chapter, 1970). He also translates from Slavic languages.

Slaviček is a rationalist and nonconformist in his poetry. His poems resemble prose, yet they are not devoid of warmth. He seems to carry on a running dialogue between his fellow man and himself about the basic problems of existence, bringing out the absurd details of everyday life and giving them poetic luminosity.

A LITTLE POEM ABOUT LOVE

At the end you will be only a poem
and a memory when I am ill: in darkness, half an hour
                    before midnight
when the city roars outside in the fog
You will be a small friendship with the World
You will give a needed charm to this or that facade
                    once and somewhere
to this or that place deserted and without traces
in the shadow of a journey when a good and quiet
                    sea plays on the walls
in a shadowy afternoon: I tell you, everything else is in vain.

Mihailovich

THE CITY LOVES ME SO
WHEN IT IS DESERTED AND WHITE

The city loves me so when it is deserted and white
and the dear streets sleep under the snow as if non-existent
they only kiss me softly with their silence and silence
as when she and I were most alone
the city loves me when it is deserted
the city loves me it wants something
I cannot help it nor can it help me
no gentle help can we offer each other
dear streets and I
but as we wait for her
we listen to each other
and the clock strikes
and the steps crunch as they return

Mihailovich

ONCE MORE WE TALKED A LONG TIME I AND THE RIVER

Once more we talked for a long time I and the river
quietly and somewhat confidentially and forever,
I did not like it. Especially not
that noisy and navigable water that flows.
I will remain on my shore. I will gaze into the distance.
Behind my back there will be houses houses houses
and the daylight. And distant mountains and brooks,
and quiet immense seas ruffled by the wind.
But I will be able to lean on .very little.

Mihailovich

IMAGINATION (DEEP IN THE TWENTIETH CENTURY A.D.)

In the sweat of my brow I toss from side to side
lying on my back: prophets and founders of religions
            spoke about it
surveying the situation, without suggesting
            the getting up or a better couch.
They did not forget that I was a man, they emphasized that
            each in his own way
(somewhat anxiously and with qualifications)
but I liked very few of them.
Even reformers and statesmen, oh and the military leaders,
and merchants, of course,
intervened long ago,
the affair became more and more complicated,
revolutionaries came to say their piece too.
And I lay there extending my arms, attempting to reach,
            to throw away—
I recited poems (and curses), saw tall, soft flags
and I still do that and I still do that, weak, even forgotten
(in the sweat of my brow, tossing from side to side)
but I am already rather old and wondrously huge
and the game continues (but history and days are adorned
            with loud plumage).
In the process, screws and entire plates of uninterrupted
            progress fall on me.
It is about time they celebrate my patience also.

Mihailovich

AT LAST IT IS TIME FOR MAN TO HAPPEN

At last it is time for Man to happen
(and Man is not custom but wish he is not a director but a friend)
for his desire and spirit to happen
for his Exit to happen: his brotherhood and activity
It is time for love to happen
for the Journey to happen
for essence to happen
It is time for undisguised suffering to happen
and not for dying and enduring and encouraging
Time for the sea to be dense and full of quiet glitter
for a shore to be a shore and not a nondeparture
for flowers to smell for slopes to be slopes and not positions
for plains to be plains and not property
and for waters to be full of currents
Time for us to dwell all over the world
to embrace the Earth as a mother
to choose trains as we like, stations at the spur of the moment
to observe and hear lights
to listen to our own unboundedness and to speech no one utters
Time for us to compose difficult sonnets
Time for us to fraternize rules and humanity
laws and integrity
Time for us to fraternize roads and life

Or the time is not yet and never will be.

Mihailovich

MERRYMAKING

The exploration of space and microcosm
Then again popular music
Headlines about bombing and rebellions
Then again popular music
A meeting about an individual in a crowd and about
    a writer as a free spirit
Then again popular music
Contemplation about love, actually about that woman
    or those evenings yesterday and the day before yesterday
Then again popular music
The twilight with a breeze and old religions
Then again popular music
The problem of overpopulation and future cities
Then again popular music
The eighth lecture about mental hygiene and the fifteenth
    about abundant moral deviations
Then again popular music
Contemporary language in life and literature
Then again popular music
The history of my people and its cultural heritage
Then again popular music and cheap movies

One might even think we are very gay.

Mihailovich & Moran

SLAVKO MIHALIĆ 1928–

Slavko Mihalić was born in 1928 in Karlovac, Croatia. As a journalist, he came to Zagreb, where he worked as an editor and publisher. He was the editor of *The Bridge*, a periodical in foreign languages. He was also the secretary of the Union of Yugoslav Writers and of the Union of Croatian Writers.

He has published several books of verse since 1943: *Komorna muzika* (Chamber Music, 1954), *Put u nepostojanje* (Journey into Non-existence, 1956), *Početak zaborava* (Beginning of Oblivion, 1957), *Darežljivo progonstvo* (Generous Exile, 1959), *Godišnja doba* (The Seasons, 1961), *Ljubav za stvarnu zemlju* (Love for the Real Land, 1964), *Prognana balada* (Banished Ballad, 1965), *Jezero* (A Lake, 1966), and *Posljedna večera* (The Last Supper, 1968).

In his poetry, Mihalić exhibits neo-romantic and intellectualistic inclinations, attempting to overcome the absurdity of life with his ardent belief in the humanistic role of a poet. Writing in an idiom remarkable for its simplicity, precision, and lyrical fluency, he is considered one of the best of contemporary Croatian poets.

A BANISHED BALLAD

To my mother, my father

It happened unexpectedly
The south wind was in the air
Autumn resembled spring
It happened with the sun's smile
on the lips

That man, otherwise with a back huge
As a mountain
Otherwise, with a whirl of wisdom in his eyes

Otherwise, with hands as heavy as thunder
One could hear the blow of his fist a long time

That man, on that strange day
I say: a girl unbuttoned
Her shirt
(She stared through the window
Instead of into the mirror)
I say: on the shore a pussy willow
Had opened up

He resounded from his innermost being
But he dispersed all the clouds.

He started to sing in such a harmonious voice
The street was stunned (as if it had lost
Its dress)

First out of shame
Then out of enormous joy

An orange vendor opened wide
The door of his shop

And still he was not satisfied
And still he was not satisfied
He had not had enough
And he wrote above the door
Take what belongs to you

But after the night that followed
After minutes in dark evening suits
After seconds with cylinders and bamboo
Sticks

The accursed northwind blew
The girl buttoned up her shirt
Catkins fell off the willow trees

The merchant went to serve his customers

Starting with the suburbs
And that man who sang
Reduced to a microbe
And slavishly immobilized

Was banned

Well, someone had to pay

Malby

METAMORPHOSIS

I would like to know from where
this emptiness comes, so that
I turn into a transparent lake in which
you can see the bottom, but without fish.

But without shells, crabs, without
underground growth that at least
has a name, and I am today
nameless. Even a little nonexistent.

And so, speaking of emptiness, I move
the water in the lake, it throws around
sand and some tiny particles
clinging to the bottom. I am becoming ill.

I walk the streets with my head bent like
another lake, dark above all, and even
poisonous; let us not talk about those
repulsive beings that crawl at the bottom, so
that now I stink to myself.

Mihailovich & Moran

THE APPROACHING OF THE STORM

Look at those clouds, Vera, why are you silent
For God's sake I am not a beast, but here is the rain
How suddenly it turned cold
We are far from the city

All right, Vera, I'll never forget your presents
We are now one, and why speak
Yellow clouds usually bring on a hail
Already everything is silent, the crickets and wheat

If you wish we could remain
I am afraid for you; as for myself, it is the same
Lightning is dangerous in the fields
And we are now the tallest (and so damned alone)

Many a farmer will lament tonight over the grain
    spilled from the wheat
I don't want to depend so much on the changes
Don't cry, Vera, that is only the nerves
They too forebode the storm

I'm telling you, life is much simpler in every respect
Here are the first drops, now all hell will break loose
Button up your dress, look, the blossoms are already closing
I could not forgive myself if something should
    happen to you

Of course this place will remain sacred in my memory
Please hurry and don't turn back

Mihailovich & Moran

LITTLE FUGUE

Not even the stone endured; not even memory.
We shall go on with wounded butterflies and stooped ants
Not even the sky with its glorious centuries
Just hold my hand as tightly as you can
We must pull through this night
Or this day, it's the same, this rending apart
When not one bird recalls its song
Your blood is feverish your hand so cold
Blind apparitions move beside us
Our bodies will save us in love
They only know their own laws
Not even the river with its sand; not even the forest
Not even the snake now rotted; not even the weasel
The sun's askew as if hung from a rope
The moon and all the stars lie between the teeth of a beast
Here is our bed among these sharp rocks
Each of your kisses is a cup of blood
Never before has love been so generous

Nejgebauer & Zion

OUR ANCIENT FAMILY SIGN

Traveling thus with a jug of fierce wine
I embraced fat matrons in pretty daydreams

My soul sang in a cage gone rusty
With cardboard sword I cut the thieves down

Who wouldn't ask to have that life all over
Penniless it seemed I had bought everything

And above the door our ancient family sign
Black gallows and a greasy rope.

Simic

RUNNING

Always the same road rain flash of lightning
Barefoot boy soldier singer all at once
Lover searching for his bed through the mist
The posse of waves drunken orgy of crows above
I kept running over the sand while I did other things
Let cities go to ruin behind my back
With the wind in pack the prow of the wolves' flight
Over by the dunes the review of corpses
Next to the shucked-corn some other hungry army
Wedding of smoke hearth and cannons
Ceaselessly resound throughout my bones
As I fall down and keep on running
Drunken fisherman holding a tatter of his net
At each step the saints kick him with their heels
If he stops the dogs will get him
One bloody stone per each step
And a young woman with her breasts bared
Will the bough get her the wandering hunter
By the lake that ascends from Hell
Sly lake with a noose of pearls
Lake of shallow hopes and bottomless betrayals
I who haven't turned around yet
Who am fear embodied I this small universe
I scorned the fruit that wrestles with worms
Next to the dread of fishes and chained hands of clams
Next to a mother with her child and a destroyed hut
Injustice you are constant like breathing
I jumped over the glassy sands like over embers
Tomorrow and yesterday harmoniously mixed
Who would separate the years so happily coupled
Out of their bellies the centuries wail to each other
The sky has strewn itself over the clouds
Show me the difference belfries and gallows
Hear the drum-roll the human bones tolling alarm
It doesn't reach even to the top of the poplars
While in the sky the stars graze peacefully

Before they lower themselves in milky ripples
And kiss the sinners where it's sweetest to kiss
But I kept running to remember I didn't manage
Running I ate and raped at times
I was even born running
With a cry following the dazed millions
Falling dead and I broke in half and ran in pair
The whole history falters in my knees
The unborn hang and are given rifles
The lovers separated hungry chained
Blowing on empty fingers swollen ear-drums
By the lakes trenches graves
Steadily heavier and darker in hope
Furrowed gouged like this frescoe
Over the white length of the treacherous sand.

Simic

PASTORAL

My world is small
Yet when I plunge in it
It seems bottomless

At times I rule there
At times it eludes me skillfully
Then I call it with a flute

But it happens that I play the wrong song
Then strange sounds are heard
Little demons descend

When goat paths come to the end
Chasms open before me
Cold winds brush against me

The little demons

Run entangled
In sky or on earth

Surely a bad end
But I hear a goat's bell
Right behind my back.

Simic

FEAST FULL OF EXPECTATION

I drank this wine already, sat here
Neither younger nor older (does the spirit count)
Raised my glass thus a little above my head
Waiting for the miracle whenever it pleases.

Precious liquid, as long as it is not used,
Pours betrayed like rain from the roof.

Tomorrow again the sun will rise to the level
Of this glass, this feast full of expectation.

Behind our backs someone mighty mocks us,
Innocent, though, like a housewife plucking a rooster.

Yes, just this fair, this dreamy music,
One could see from the corner of the eye at times
All seas, lands throwing themselves into the offing.

How wide is the palm of the hand?
Enough for us to search for each other hopelessly.

Simic

ALONE, FOR SUCH IS THE VICTORY

No longer fear; wolf's teeth I feel showing.
No longer the road, God no; in the meadow the bushes call me.
If my eyes glow, the crows flap with contempt.
No longer memory; noble human ancestry.

Not houses, pavements or lender's establishments,
Endlessly hungry breast reaching up after the snow.

And I will not get lost: the winds tell me
That my target is on the other side.

How beautifully grins the lantern of my wolf's eye.
No longer time; my steps advance at double pace.

Hunters, already tonight I'll arrive
On the meadow that ate the tracks of the betrayer,
Calling to my mighty self in the heavens,
Alone, for such is the victory.

Simic

THE LAST ADVENTURE

He is now a ruler in the country that once exiled him
Neither king nor king's minister, he simply asserts his will,
Observing from the window how drugged people walk the streets
Wise and handsome, for he has freed himself from a purpose

Yes, he is now like a child; and at the same time like a tombstone
Sometimes it seems to him that besides two hands he also has two wings
But he won't fly; he knows it is not enough to feel
As the sea feels omnipotent and yet does not change the contours of the
     land

The greatest adventure is a flower in a glass of water
With supreme effort he pressed into it all his beliefs
And now deeply just, leaning, he waits for it to wither
Peacefully as when one shakes off the cigarette ash.

Mihailovich & Moran

FISHING

The water flows as if carried by someone
Whether clear or flooding the shores, it is indifferent
Peacefully time grazes everywhere the same
The mountain too will some day fall

We entered the water to our waist—enraged butchers
On the shore women shivered from hunger
There wind assailed our distorted faces
Our howling was heard far off

For the fish the net is no novelty
Always between the shores, the surface and the bottom
We went heavy, with headache and bloodshot eyes
Like after drinking but the drinking was yet to come

All night we shed that cold colorless blood
Senseless we dug our hands deeper than allowed
Die, water!—it did not even hear us
Leaving us frozen above the corpses

Mihailovich & Moran

JOVAN HRISTIĆ 1933–

A native of Belgrade, Jovan Hristić studied literature at
the University of Belgrade. He has occupied numerous
positions with periodicals and publishing houses. He is
now an editor in Belgrade's leading publishing house
Nolit.

He writes poetry, drama, and essays. His books of
poetry include: *Dnevnik o Ulisu* (Ulysses' Diary, 1954),
Pesme (Poems, 1959), and *Aleksandrijska škola* (The
Alexandrian School, 1963). He has translated widely,
especially from English literature.

Hristić represents the Anglo–Saxon and neo–classical
tradition in contemporary Serbian poetry. Contemplative, rationalistic, and erudite, he prefers philosophical
themes and contemporary problems such as alienation
and loneliness. Even when he employs classical motifs he
does so in order to illuminate modern problems.

TO PHAEDRUS

This too I want you to know, my dear Phaedrus, we lived
In hopeless times. From tragedy
We made comedy, from comedy tragedy.

But the important: seriousness, measure, wise exaltedness
And exalted wisdom, always escaped us. We were
On no-one's land, neither ours alone,

Nor someone else's; always a few steps removed
From what we are, from what we ought to be.

O my dear Phaedrus, while you stroll
With virtuous souls on the island of the blessed,
Recall at times our name:

Let its sound spread in the resonant air,

Let it rise toward this heaven it could never reach
So that at least in your conversation our souls find rest.

Simic

THAT NIGHT THEY ALL GATHERED ON THE HIGHEST TOWER

That night they all gathered on the highest tower:
Astronomers, mathematicians, one of the magi from Syria,
To read in the stars the glory of the King of Kings,
And demonstrate his immortality in geometric manner.

Just before dawn, they nodded their heads
In consent to each other's thoughts. The answer of the stars
Was positive. The bugles announced
The glory of the King of Kings to the breaking day.

In the palace, at the feast table, they were awaited
By the one to whom the stars gave their word tonight,
And whose future overflowed like fresh wine,
Which in the golden chalices awaited the toasts.

Only one among them, some youth, who just mastered geometry,
Was not fully convinced by what they read in the stars:
For the stars always give their answers to mortals,
But to what question, only they know.

Simic

ISLANDS

Again the season comes for me to turn the pages of his book:
And sudden rains sweep away feelings of winter
Like sand which winds have carried to the rooftops,
When walking through grass trousers become heavy with water.

Can this be some old fever left by February
forgotten in my bones? Or is it the flapping of sails
from some long-over dream? Come then. Drops from the leaves
And lovers laughing in abandoned bowers.

Footsteps pass. The sea breaks against cliffs.
In the small hours and wiser after rain
Sea gropes toward stone. Waves roll up
On to the seashore. Women turn in bed.
The wind is off the islands. Rain falls out at sea.

Darkness. In the harbor hausers chafe the deck.
Do these islands still come to you in your dreams?
The window is open, summer enters the room
Traversing the flimsy curtain of memories, memories.

Hristíc & Johnson

IVAN V. LALIĆ 1931–

Ivan V. Lalić was born in Belgrade, where he finished law shool. He spent a few years in Zagreb, and now works in Belgrade as an editor.

Lalić began to publish poetry in 1952. His first book, *Bivši dečak* (The Boy That Was) appeared in 1955. Among his other books of poetry are: *Argonauti i druge pesme* (Argonauts and Other Poems, 1961), *Vreme, vatre, vrtovi* (Time, Fires, Gardens, 1961), *Čin* (The Act, 1963), *Izabrani stihovi* (Selected Verses, 1969), and *Smetnje na vezama* (Interference in Connections, 1975).

He is a poet of subdued pathos and great technical skill, inclining toward classical motifs and intellectualism, who creates a poetry that is both complex and refined.

THE KING AND THE SINGER

You have to be the stronger one—
My destiny is to endure this song,
this fire, this clownsuit of poetry,

and peer into your squinting eyes,
into that wrath that boils up
and cools down like some unstable metal
in the gusty yards of your smelters.

So I go round and round you
like rain in the desert,
and we are both enchanted:
You in your strength,
I in my inwardness—
and the game goes on through every song—

Every song in which your appetite
sees roses or the delicate forged gold
of vowels, and I my death.

Because—always—
in the space between two words,
an empire awakens, unfamiliar,
suddenly disturbed, explosive
like an anthill struck by a spark.

And so in the end, your Excellency,
we are powerless, both of us:
From the wedding of this song
comes a heaven, a more dangerous earth,
and the multitudes we cannot control.

And every night
the familiar stars
slip further and further away.

Truesdale

from KALEMEGDAN

All my dead in this wind,
the fourth night now, and the fifth
and my window is
the whipped eye of a horse.

All my dead in this wind—
the leaves, the dust, the years,

and my mouth is full
of blood and tenderness,
my tongue pierced by the golden pin
my mother searched for once
in a dream.

The fourth night now, and the fifth—
wind around the house,
a clean dry flame,

and I drift on an insomnia
lighter than air,
unlocking names,
justifying a world
I did not create.

I defend myself. I exist.

Truesdale

VOICES OF THE DEAD

from the cycle *Melisa*

I

Voices of the dead. They are not dead. Who hears
The dead? Rain on the bronze gates of the morning.
The freshness of wild gardens keeping doves
In the cobwebs of roses. I was that emptiness between them.

I was on a bank of a river lost for days, hours.
It doesn't matter. In time beyond this time.
And the river is wide, river from the blood of ancestors.
How to swim up its stream? Who has reached its mouth?

O dead ones, by this river I found a roofless house.
House left in a hurry and a thin thread of smoke
Woven into a mist that grows thicker and thicker.

A house uncompleted. Then winter began.
A window frightened by the strength of a storm woke me up.
Voices of the dead. They are not dead. Who hears them?

II

In the night a distant fire blazes. Then another.
Butterflies of flame settle the edge of the night.
A third fire. Soon a clear line of fire

Completed. Ring of sleep. Nobody gets through.

Chestnuts shake off their leaves in fear.
Men say: Autumn. Melisa, it is the camp
Of a great dead army, settled on a distant hill.
Alone, breathless and troubled I hear the bugler.

Instead of ringing brass, I hear early snows
Falling in empty woods. The fires remain.
When the earth smooths a wrinkle on its forehead,

Entire towns collapse. The fires remain.
Ring around sleep. Has anyone heard the bugler?
The bugler beyond silence and the silence stronger.

IV

Voices of the dead remain. Distant voices. Who hears
The dead? Perhaps, the color of old gold
And the foam of dark sea. Perhaps, like a storm
Lacking space. Perhaps, hushed after an illness.

Unknown. It doesn't matter. Perhaps, soiled by war,
Dust. Or with a quiet noise like a seashell
Placed against the ear in a burning summer afternoon.
It doesn't matter. Voices beyond this game. Kindred words.

The buzzing of the spindle in the fairy lullaby
From a pure age. Dream disguised into an event.
Voices of the dead. Still they are not dead.

I lie in the night. Awake. Quiet. They are quieter.
I fall asleep and dream of drums. Ancient drums.
Great dark drums broken and left in the rain.

Simic

MARINA II

We linger awhile
in this silence, waiting perhaps
the pure wrath which,
being in us already, is not coming.

It is like fire
in the salt-blood of the sea,
the wild seed in the red dust
which I spit into like an Indian
and knead into the god,
into this wild rose, and this dream
of a white-hot bee
with a sterile, diamond sting.

In this silence of the beach
these echoes bead out like sweat,
these images
where blossoms of foam
tremble along the littered shore,
a dream on the lashes of the sea
heavy with salt for all our wounds:

Here the bones of a bird
still charmed in the symmetry of flight;
there some empty cans, their surface
a garden of rust roses
like a frail handkerchief stained
with blood wiped from a face—

a scattering of signs
and our voices mixed like blood,
like the smells of lovers, like history—

angry words, emerging like the stars
on the right, in the expected place.

Truesdale

BYZANTIUM II

The strategist over a map
and his legislator. Gold sand
in the hourglass:

Ripeness gleams in the eyes
of children, and wisdom in their games
under the cypresses.
Tiny blades of grass burn away
the inscriptions from the stone
and the sky repeats them by heart.

At noon, cupolas flame in your eye
and mirror themselves all over
the city. The sea in the foreground,
snow on the frontiers (where footprints
of wolves mingle with those of strangers).
A seal on a letter, in the signet ring
the movement of a dead hand.
Processions wind along the walls
in the glory of a borderless moment
and the bee above his flower
buzzes with antiquity.
A star drops its winged shadow
like an anchor or a gull
into the shallow sea. The struggle goes on:

To bear the loneliness,
to bear this exchange of splendor
for barbarity, and to gain nothing—
not even freshness—in return,
to bear without relief
the weight of this heavy solemn
sentence.

Language, more and more indefinite,
celebrates the movement of its creation
exiled into the center of a pure
lost circle. Wind at the frontiers.
Spearpoints of land throwing off sparks
in the afternoon sea.
The strategist over his map,
a scribe over a treatise on duration.

The eyes of the basilisk flame
in the blackberry bush. The hunter
nearly dead from concentration
carefully moves his mirror:
Snake tongue, cock's crest,
and the final look of eye into eye,
like a strange reward
at the end of a forced temptation.

A guard at the Gate
crosses himself mechanically.
Chains are drawn across
the night harbor. In the emperor's room
a candle burns low.

The Almighty One in the gold luxury
of his dome, in the magnificence
of his pure absence,
repeats a gesture of true benediction.

And the night which is coming
will be longer than all nights,
and its power to endure lost
in the account of the struggle:

When ripeness returns the glance
of its own image, it is as dangerous,
without the mirror, without the ruse,
as the first beast in the first morning
of creation.

Truesdale

SPRING LITURGY FOR BRANKO MILJKOVIĆ 1934–61

I

Are you really alone now, Branko?
Alone enough to say to the earth:
Here is another name for memory,
a new feast for your despair
when, in the spring,
you have to be a miracle again?
Alone enough for all that was
inside of you to echo beautifully
in the empty vaults of your blood?
Can you reflect at last the fire
of that still undescribed star
which turns the same corner
where yesterday you were
and silence is today?

Because you always wanted
that solitude—to be alone
and heavy with that exact moment
in the night when blood and time
merge quickly like powerful rivers.

Are you really alone now
and stronger than any temptation?
Or does the red clay taste already
like summer's ore of light?
Do you recognize in the air above you
the first scattering of green signs?

Do you hear again
those words that overpower you
and tear that brief repose
from your eyelids, like the skin
of leaf-buds?

Look, dying was no solution to death—
you summon in vain the angel
with your silence, tall as the cry
of a falconer. All questions are the same—
any time of the year the sea roars,
and fire descends always the same path.

Now is your time to go further—
all the voices of the earth
are erect in your ear
and tremble on long stems,
the breezes lift the pages
and we repeat in you:
when a poet dies he proves
that birds fly and death cannot exist.

II

Do not lament my disarmed voice
that cannot stop this spring with words.
I know it has always been,
that tomorrow's rain will fill up the lake
of what we hear this morning,
that yesterday's bird brings me news
of all floods, of every leafing branch.

If this is a dream
don't ever wake me.
Dispersed like fire in a wind
I dream myself, and that air you breathe
(already moist with summer) bears
like an ancient veil
the imprint of my face.

Everything I am dreaming
is somewhere completed
in a motion, a shadow, a mountain,
a rebellion.

Less and less I remember your faces,
less and less your words,
that arrangement of voices along
the empty squares of a chessboard.
Yet everything—
star, flower, wind, seasons—
has still the same position
and the sea that welcomes you
belongs still to me.

Perhaps this is the way
to remember beauty, to achieve the poem,
to dream the word to its end.

Look, yesterday's bird
brings me news of all floods,
of every leafing branch—
let me dream, and doubt, and burn away—
do not lament my disarmed voice.

III
Tree in the wind
remembered like a letter,
tree in the wind
that will blaze like charcoal,
tree in the wind
cast like lead and printed
onto a dull gray sky,
tree, tree,
rude sign of the earth
in a windy landscape—
O deaf, mute tree
between two fields of wheat,

sign of defective memory:
the poem lives in a forgotten place
where fire barely burns—
the sea has its origins,
and the shape of the first tree
in the raw air imitates
beneath the bark the lost star
returning, visible, from oblivion.

Tree in the wind
first syllable of dawn—
a bird dreams in the sea,
and words in the well
of a child's tears.
And still, a poem is a poem
even when it is made of earth,
and fire is fire
even without its sparks:
in water, in sand, in loss
the fire rekindles itself.
The order of stars survives
the ruin of the star-gazers
and their towers.
Silence circles the poem
and knots together the words,
and life repeats itself like spring.
Before the lightning of loss
it narrows like an eye,
or crashes like the sea
before the deaf citadel of land.

But the edge of each shore the sea
awakens is already proclaimed
on the damp wind:
the skin of erect vision bursts,
o tree in the wind, the fire dawns—
on the edge of the first leaf
which no longer remembers

a beginning or an end
and marvels only at its shape.

Tree in the wind,
letter in a brief word
it is trying to finish
like a covenant—
tree that stutters with arms
full of living rain.

Beauty goes on—who cares
that it remembers itself or not?
The road goes on over the broken miles.
In truth, there is no death;
in truth the bird flies;
and the great delusion
is the body laid out in death.
Tree in the wind,
you naked sign of the powerful earth,
you spread your leaves like a flag—
you are the sentry-tower
of the battle already decided;
your root touches the cornerstone
of loss; the air changes your pronunciation,
and every spring asserts the Mediterranean.
The sea awakes beyond the deaf rocks,
the bird inscribes its song
around the nest—
tree in the wind,
o word, o instant of wisdom,
here beauty returns like an invasion,
and the sea glitters .
with stars and stars.

Simic & Truesdale

DUBRAVKO ŠKURLA 1933–57

Dubravko Škurla was born in 1933 in Preko near Zadar. He started to write poetry in 1947, but wrote his best poems in the year or two before his suicide in 1957. He never saw any of his nearly 800 poems published in book form. Two collections, *Dvije obale* (Two Shores, 1967) and *Kameni brid* (The Stone Edge, 1970), were published posthumously.

Škurla's poems are characterized by distinct originality, fine sensitivity, and modernistic tendencies. A combination of a confessional approach and somewhat naive surrealism, revealing a fascination with the world around him, and a touch of sadness, points to the poet's great potential, which probably was never fully realized because of his untimely death.

DISQUIET BECAUSE OF THE HORSEMEN

I was at the seashore
     which turned cruel,
     uncertain in warmth and color,

And when I thought that
     nothing else could
     happen,

Three horse tails
     painfully whipped me,
and three unknown horsemen,
     who rode here
     from different directions,
went through me, the empty space;

Nevertheless I became so heavy

that I could no longer touch
my left hand with my right.

Mihailovich & Moran

I WROTE A WORD AND IT TURNED BLACK

I wrote a word and it turned
     black,
somewhere a child was singing
     as if from another
     world.
I searched for a blue mirror
     of a small lake
     with a live bottom,
to look at myself in it
fearing the reflection.

Distant one, could your face
     return to the world the depth
     of perspective.

The clouds stand dead
     as on photographs.
I think they are pinned
     to this curdled crust
     of the earth,
to this stone in the mouth.

Mihailovich & Moran

TWO SHORES

I looked for you in the night
        full of stars
        naked
and found the stars,
I looked for you on the terraces
        of southern cafes
        under street lamps
and soaked in multicolored lights
        I looked for you in the smell
        of the stone and in the depth
        of the earth
and found a herd of small ants
        that were doing
        their chores

Mihailovich & Moran

CENE VIPOTNIK 1914–72

Cene Vipotnik was born in Zagorje ob Savi, Slovenia. He graduated from the University of Ljubljana. During the last war he was interned in Italy. Although he had been active in cultural affairs since the war and had appeared with his first poems even before the war, he published only one book of verse—*Drevo na samem* (A Lonely Tree, 1956). He also translated, mostly from the French. He was a professor and editor in a leading Slovenian publishing house.

Vipotnik's earlier poetry concerns itself with the here and now of the real world, and it is characterized by fine sensitivity and pronounced lyricism. In his poetry written during the war, the brutal reality penetrates the poet's secluded world and makes his poetry brittle and harsh. His later poems turn, for the most part, to love and the changes love evokes in the poet.

HARD TIMES

The yard is quandrangular. Solitude dwells here.
My sight now slams against the wall—too high,
now avidly kisses all silent, all gloomy skies.
Beyond the wall a tree unfurled its branches up into the heights;
this side it disrobes as winds rush through it, as rains wash it—
for autumn covers everything again with its weary mistiness.

Long ago a war broke out: it stabbed the wall,
left gaping shot wounds and, crossways, heaped barbed wire
where distant fields and green pastures sleep forgotten;
it cracked the native land, split the people, things, cattle . . .
We suffer and wait for happiness. Happiness and death.

The yard is quadrangular. Solitude dwells here.
The winds churn the clouds, the rains rush softly
to the evening, descending lower and lower like a lonely crow.

In an unseen tower bells are ringing across darkening roofs.
Children's cries rise from the yard: they are playing hostages.

The screaming children press into a line and shoot and shoot.
They put a child to the wall—hey! he just began to walk—
he meekly shuffles from foot to foot and rubs his numbed hands,
and, like condemned souls, leaves fly down from the chestnut tree,
children trample them into the mud and shout: "Well, fall! Fall!"
   to the child,
but the child stands and kneads his small, cold hands,
glances at the window where a solitary light expelled the dark . . .
ah, the child stands and . . . does not fall.

In an unseen tower bells ring through rainy darkness,
dark leaves flutter through the dreaming night.
I feel them wetly glide over my naked heart.

Oh, let us turn the leaf!

Zrimc

BURIAL

A concentration camp sketch

Hut no. 6. The door is gaping wide.
The cowering sky is perching on the roof.
The rain stitches on outside.
The silent crowd gathers to say goodby.
Someone who slipped into the blessed darkness
Is borne with homely rite in earth to lie.

The chilly silence petrifies each face.
Too small a coffin here for him was found;
Even in the grave he will be short of space.
Over its end his clayey feet stick out
As if to cry: we still might tread the ground.

And when they lay him down on the black carriage
(we hear the muttered miserere read)
Hark to the beaked cadaver's bony cackle
"Look, friends, I'm dead!"

We stand alone under the darkening sky.
O life, where are you? Let the birds of death
Be overpowered by your splendid flight!

Shrouded in peace, past the sharp compound wires
Our lonely brother into the dark mist goes.
The men stand numb, rage hissing in their souls.

Into the soundless night the black hearse rolls.

MacKinnon

IVAN SLAMNIG 1930–

Ivan Slamnig was born in 1930 in Metković, Croatia. He graduated from the University of Zagreb and now teaches comparative literature at that university.

He has published the following books of verse: *Aleja poslije svečanosti* (The Avenue After Celebration, 1956), *Odron* (Landslide, 1956), *Naronska siesta* (Siesta in Narona, 1963), *Monografija* (A Monograph, 1965), and *Limb* (Limbo, 1968). He also writes prose and critical essays, and translates from English, French, and Russian.

Slamnig often uses a prosaic tone in his poems in order to play with the serious problems of life, to point out the supremacy of reason, and to experiment in form. Primarily intellectually inclined, he folllows the Anglo-Saxon tradition in Croatian poetry. He is urbane and slightly ironic, emphasizing the drawbacks of modern civilization with its fetish of technology. His translations from English and other languages have undoubtedly molded to a certain degree his poetic personality.

★   ★   ★

An at random hurriedly gathered small company
was suffused with whiskey
and just as we wanted to say something
some prankster pulled out an old watch
whose chain coldly and brightly rang,
played the first melody,
again we wanted to say something
and that bloke he again pulled on the chain
and the watch rang once more
this time a different melody
which resembled a polka
as the earlier one resembled a waltz
in order to speak we heard it out

and opened our mouths but again he pulled
one otherwise charming minuet
as all minuets are
especially those of old clocks
we listened to two more melodies
since the old watch held five
and just as we were about to say something
the watch was again wound up
and again the waltz played
then the polka
then the minuet
and the other two melodies
again.

Mihailovich & Moran

THE LATE COMING HOME

Bitter, rather dry in our mouths
the taste, and we go to bed
imagining a dove,
never able to fancy
its beak or head or one wing,
any of red talons,

and cupping it in our palms
we ponder what kind of a beak or head,
a wing or what talon
this bird should have.
So sleep surprises us
like children after crying.

Mihailovich & Wright

A SAILOR

In front of the inn we saw a sailor.
He drank his beer from a particularly large mug.
He sat facing each one of us,
and the waitress liked him too.
He explained
how he always carries his house with him
and showed a purple tatooed house
baring his chest.
He laughed
and looked at all of us
ready to receive kindness, ready to pay a fine,
he set his feet firmly on the ground
(in case it began to sway).
He was still fighting the sea
and we hid with our palms
our small-flame anxiousness.

Mihailovich & Wright

THE POINT IS TO STOP THE HORSE

The point is to stop the horse.
Huge and brown, it gallops, not too swiftly,
out from the road's grey ribbon, overgrown with thorn bushes,
bridled, saddled, riderless.

I calculate the motions and figure out everything:
how I shall catch him and with all my weight press
   on the reins,
and then pat him with my left hand on the neck,
   to quiet him down.

So. Now. I lift my right arm but note that it reaches only
    to the elbow,
lift my left arm but it hangs stiff.
I lack knees, a part of my shoulder, a shoulder blade,
and all my hair.

Mihailovich & Moran

SIESTA AT NARONNA

A small white colonnade.
See him pass from column to column,
His eyes are wild, his coat is the yellow lynx;
Now, as I look at him, he moves
Away from the column and along the horizon
And is hidden again by a column.
See, see how tall he is, how beautiful;
See how wild he is, ah how wild he is;
See his black hair, look how he looks.
He might be some Vardeus
Or some other wild tribe,
Daorseus, Naresius,
Delmata, Croata.
(I watch him eating a grape
On my stone terrace
Girdled with its white colonnade)

What did he come for, Drusus,
With sheaf and bow
In his coat of fur?
He came, Drusilla,
He came to buy
The blade of a spear or the barb of an arrow,
Poison and something funny for his children.
What did he come for, Drusus?
He came, Silla,
For tattoo needles
For helmet and buckle;
He came, baby,

To choose a stone from our facade,
To take a column from our colonnade
Glittering like a stalactite;
He came to pinch a god of our house
Just for the fun of it,
He came to rob us
To beat us to death
And not to give a damn.

Mortimer

ANTUN ŠOLJAN 1932–

Born in 1932 in Belgrade, Antun Šoljan studied at the University of Zagreb and later became a freelance writer, a prolific translator, and an editor of books and anthologies.

Among his many books are the collections of poetry *Na rubu svijeta* (At the Edge of the World, 1956), *Izvan fokusa* (Out of Focus, 1957), *Gartlic za čas kratiti* (Miscellany to Kill Time, 1965), and *Gazela i druge pjesme* (A Gazelle and Other Poems, 1970). Šoljan has written short stories, novels, plays, critical essays, and has translated copiously from English, American, German, and Russian literature. He is one of the most active authors in contemporary Croatian literature.

Together with Slamnig, Šoljan represents the Anglo-Saxon tradition in contemporary Yugoslav poetry, although he is less cerebral and more experimental. He is also more interested in creating myths, in expressing his views on the dilemmas of modern man, and in revealing contradictions inherent in ideas and in life. Although he is more and more preoccupied with other genres, Šoljan still manages to keep step with developments in modern poetry, as shown in his last collection.

STONE THROWER

I

I run out barefooted to the river bank,
to the river bank with a thousand herons,
I run out, stop, and stand on tip-toes,
to look up and down the bank,
although I have a hundred times before,

although I have a hundred times looked,
although nothing has ever changed,
since I started throwing long stones

with a fine and skilled long arm,
on the bank full of identical stones,
black and round to kill herons.

It seems, by the clouds, already autumn.

And so in the eternally alike mornings,
before the eternally alike stones on the river bank,
although I'm skilled and know how to throw,
although I have a hundred times before,
although I have a hundred times raised my hand,
I stand and hesitate, I stand and do not throw,
although it is autumn and herons will fly away.

I stand and do not throw, for I must hit,
I do not throw for I might miss
the heron which I must hit,
the only heron that belongs to me,

although I have a hundred times sworn
not to recognize

certain entirely imaginary laws.

II

And so I, the best thrower of them all,
the most skillfully skilled man who knows his trade,
who could build a mountain
out of dead and wet herons
and wear a coat of heron's feathers
and have long heron's wings
on the wooden wall above the door,

and so I, the best thrower of them all,
I bend down every time, pick up a stone,
no matter which stone on the river bank,
and wasting my strength, with trimmest swing,
with most magnificent skill I throw everywhere,

I throw everywhere about the autumn sky,
the autumn's colorless linen–like sky,
and pierce holes, through which angels

whistle street songs to me.

III

No matter which stone, Throw. Don't think about
that the stone when leaving the hand
is demented with its own life. That the strength
is not yours anymore:

that with stones you depart from here.
Hand, then a shoulder, a back and so
maybe you are not beside this river at all,

where a bent man with feeble hands
pensively picks up every so often a stone,
polished and black long stone,
weighs it in his hand and observes,
and then trembling, with care he throws
in the river and then almost stands up,
and looks up and down the river bank
whether someone has seen him,
although nothing has changed,
although for ages there's no one around.

For I have flown away with stones
and all the rest is probably the way

by which, one normally grows old.

Simic

OLD MEN

Waves throw their green thighs over the cliffs
and remain there lying like children
with orange foam around their necks.

Wind gets tied up in the fig tree, flaps his wings,
then wraps himself with a snake skin and descends
to shake hands indifferently with his new friends.

Clouds stop somewhere and tumble down like rocks,
stare in the deep blue and then freeze
into serious, cold fishermen from the north.

And so, there are too many of us now.
"Old men brood and thoughtfully chew."

Some of us, on a daily afternoon walk,
come to the end of an alley, stop in the row of trees,
raise our left arm and become a chestnut.

Some of us, when it's time, lock the doors,
so that neighbors, who are worried, in the morning enter
and see a pack of grey mice skipping away.

And some of us take off our coats, glasses and depart
so that travelers, who tail us, meet the men
who come from there and say they saw no one.

And so, one by one we go.
"Old men brood and thoughtfully chew."

Determined we pass in large wall mirrors,
on round surfaces of silver spoons,
through circling streets, around lampposts,
through streams of reddish water, through fog,
through trembling fingers and dried skeletons,

over palms, shoulders and someone's knuckles,
we pass with drums and many-colored flags;
our helmets shine and our knives. We carry plumes.

So lower the blinds to forget everything,
lower the blinds and small curtains,
since no one from the parade will remain.

"Old men brood and thoughtfully chew
Damp wool of time."

Simic

TRAVELING

After I have known all the captains by their names
and when my nails have grown long
and my eyelashes descended over my face,
on one of my long travels,

three of them, naked and brown from the sun,
and they had red scarves around their hips,
three of them resting on yellow hands,
they drank sea water on the beach,
they drank sea water and said:

"You haven't been around for a long time,
You haven't been around."

And then I swam across the seas,
and many fins passed me on the horizon.
Two inexperienced sirens lured me,
and they were young and livid like fishes,
two of them lured me and said:

"You haven't been around for a long time,
You haven't been around."

But I haven't seen the land. I was afraid,
and so I came to your country of good pines,
where I sat, nibbled the grass and caught blue fish,
lit the fire and fried my supper.

The shadows under my eyes grew deep
and I forgot travels and songs,
captains and ports and Mrs. Marie.
Weird men sat around the fire,
black bearded men sat and said:

"You haven't been around for a long time,
You haven't been around."

And so I came to your country,
why do you look at my long hair,
my long hair down to my knees?
I know Mrs. Marie has died
here among us on this bed.

I haven't been around for a long time. Mrs. Marie is gone.

I haven't been around for a long time and so I forgot
travels and songs, captains and ports
and maybe, I am not here at all.

I never went away.

Simic

KING

With good oarsmen and strong keels
my six-masted ships arrive
empty into empty harbors

for my sailors to come out and call to each other
through the hollow space between church spires
with cries of strange red birds,

for my wild horses to gallop down the highways,
for my horsemen to dismount breathing heavily
and stand silent before me without letters,

without message, instructions, aim,
my good horsemen wrapped in long green capes,
silently to grin, to laugh without a word,

for my wrestlers to go naked to the waist,
my foot soldiers, my sling throwers and others,
strong and tense, ready to kill,

for my lads to go through the fields,
through the cities, whistling monotonous songs
and embrace barren women under barren trees,

for the gun on the wall, the bugler above the harbor
to wait for the sentries to start shouting from the hills
with strange throaty voices that echo,

for the army to be armed, for the flags to unfurl
so that I may every morning lift weights
to acquire strength for unknown purpose.

Simic

VLADO GOTOVAC 1930–

Vlado Gotovac was born in 1930 in Imotski, studied philosophy at the University of Zagreb, after which he occupied positions in cultural institutions. He is now an editor at Zagreb television station.

He has been writing since 1956—poetry, stories, essays, and literary criticism. His books of verse include *Pjesme od uvijek* (Poems Forever, 1956), *Opasni prostor* (Dangerous Space, 1961), *I biti opravdan* (And To Be Justified, 1963), *Osjećanje mjesta* (The Sense of Place, 1964), *Zastire se zemlja* (The Earth Is Covered, 1967), *Približavanje* (Approaching, 1968), *Prepjevi po sjećanju* (Recasting Poems by Memory, 1968), *Čarobna špilja* (A Magic Cave, 1969), and *Sporne sandale* (Debatable Sandals, 1970).

Gotovac primarily explores man's relationship to abstract ideas. His philosophical musing sometimes forces him into hermetic situations in which he considers the fate of man and the ethereal reality of love and death.

MY SILENT BIRDS

I have lifted my eyes and nothing has filled them
My looking toward the sky is an unspeakable loss
Since no time is announced from above
The earth is covered only with clouds
And silence my heart is silent
And what I hear in the coming of birds
I see all around
Their flight and their voices have lost
What the sky has lost.

But the beating of my heart quietly sustains
That desolate sky
From which silently descend birds announcing night

And how when they once sang
  everything was visible.

Neither is anything announced in the transparent eyes of children
The golden mist from their depth is already dispersed by our wind
And their dreams are heavy, the pictures are decomposing.

Mihailovich & Moran

THE LONELY ORPHEUS

To Jura

More and more it seems that I hear the clouds
More and more my hearing attends me
The voices come from many things
I can no longer retreat into silence
I can already tell the sob of a mosquito
Or the suffering of a caught flea that trembles
More and more I do not hear the sound of man
And his words change into noise
Coming steadily from everything
A huge violin perhaps without strings
Quietly echoes across the blue sky
And the stars flicker in passion
And die down and go out and fall
While from the cool depth the new tones come
As if some drum summons for creating
The clouds carefree answer to all
And only children sing with them
More and more it seems that words are disappearing
For there is less and less of that song in them
More and more my hearing attends me
  I could descend among the dead.

Mihailovich & Moran

I GREET LIFE

To little Anna

My daughter through you I have greeted life
Like some immortal bird from an ancient fairy tale
You carry me on and on while I spend myself
I too am stronger when you are happier
Affection lifts me as I am on the road where stars were created
Joy warms with the heat that created this world
And darkness exists only for dreams quickly realized
Where I dream your pure breath burns like the bush of God
And directs my heart to transcend time
If there are no words for that, you exist
And no one could speak about my saved life
I too can walk the path of the happy people
There are no more days past, my entire life revolves around you
And in the infinite revolving is renewed from its center

I greet life

As long as I hold you in my arms I hold the world with my strength
And swaying you happily, I return the world to its carefreeness
And think if the stars collide the sound will be wonderful
And in hundreds of colors the flowers will crumble in space
As if the old gods march to coronation along a festive path
No I am not a magician but a simple worker
It is hard for me because the things I make are genuine
But I am happy because they are real for the life of everyone
For even those who do not believe me use them
And it is often easier for them since I have made them
One could dream but it is better to work on what you dream

Rain sun winds and all necessary birds and insects
That bring fertility to fields after a sterile winter
All emanate from your small hands all glow in your eyes

All rustle in your hair like the flight of the spirits
And the fruits have already conceived

I greet life

Mihailovich & Moran

A FLOWERY MANUSCRIPT

You tempt my tenderness while the wind blows
        through the tulips
Bringing their color toward my window
And through so many more flowers the colors come
        to my window
That opens like a greedy nostril over the scent
Of a dear woman

Melancholy is my tenderness that brings you
        this manuscript
And begs you to correct the errors
This gaily-colored wind is the only one
That knows the worth of guarding flowers
It rises from the garden
It flies unnoticed by the moon
It is star-studded until morning
When it comes among the flowers damp and wounded
Steeped in blood
It grows in my garden like a sunflower
Until the first cricket

This is the manuscript of my tender game
Timid like a rabbit and as harmless
And I surrender it to you as much as I love you

Mihailovich & Simic

THE CLIMBER

I, a skilful climber
on a perfect top of a steeple
which alone does not repeat
a game that is already over,
have placed a stone
with an invented name
in a secure position

and I do not have to return,
for here I have fulfilled the task
only for myself.

Mihailovich

MATEJA MATEVSKI 1929–

Mateja Matevski was born in 1929 in Constantinople into a Macedonian family. He has been one of the leading Macedonian poets since the beginning of the nineteen fifties. He has published two books of verse: *Doždovi* (Rains, 1956), and *Ramnodenica* (Equinox, 1963), and has translated French poetry.

Matevski belongs to the second generation of Macedonian postwar poets. He has contributed to the transformation of declarative, descriptive, and confessional Macedonian poetry into a meditative and abstract approach bordering at times on the surreal. Obviously influenced by French poets, he pays great attention to form, attempting to strike a balance between an abundance of impressions and an economy of expression.

from ADVENTURE

I

That sunny moment in the field by the river
took me far away
into the unknown that disappeared
I too disappeared one day
carried away by its delta.

And whatever I found
I went further away
but not for a moment away from my dark shadow
from the rebellious herb
pictured in the field by that little river.

I traveled far through the night that was decomposing
from dreams and crossroads
I filtered through my thirsty eyes
handfuls of sods and water and poems

and so much beautiful sweetness through my hungry lips
and what have I done

And I was so happy with that traveling
traveling far
into the night that was luring me.

But as soon as I stopped once to think
where I was
I remained unsated and alone on this piece of alien soil
surrounded by the storm of memories
that broke my branches.

Mihailovich

BELLS

It tolls somewhere. Somewhere far it tolls.
The peals are the gusts of the wind
which someone chases through the grass.

It tolls somewhere. On and on sharply and tenderly.
All is deaf. Only the rhythm
showers the iron shore.

It tolls somewhere. Heave me high and fathomless.
Run through the resonant cage
deafly and hopelessly.

It tolls somewhere. Tiny I toll and scream.
Everything is locked up. Bewitched
I hang on the peals.

Somewhere it tolls. Hit me. How brave and tame I am.
Time, you too lash at memories
rudely and with an endless hunger.

It tolls somewhere. Very long ago and now
Everything hurts. O sky, let me
fall to the grass of familiar peals.

Mihailovich

RAINS

I

Fear

Arrive sluggish, arrive weary horses of space,
the far-off ominous rumble of forgotten speech,
beating ceaselessly, alone, outside closed windows,
absently, with dull hooves without horseshoes,
on the slippery, on the greasy, on the peaceful earth,
beat, mingling it all darkly.

Where before this bulk, before this cotton
horizon without shape,
before this flesh of earth and night
deeply stirred and dense at the same time,
a flood upon the eyes and the spaces of death.

Where, o where, you and I, noisy and endless sea,
you monotonous
meadow horizontally tired,
longing for the vertical clarity of the wind,
where, o where,
you thick dough of rain and earth
that are to a man, that are to me
stone in the hand and mud in the eyes?

II

Song

Where do you come from, where, you familiar

never to be forgotten
song, you hopeless child, you innocent
arrow of grasses and bird of mud,
a path dusty and endless in the sun,
silvery path, restless rattlesnake,
where are you taking me?

Forever sensed in water in darkness
gentle mane, rough coarse mane
indifferently daring,
always the sinewy path of space,
like air and like the flash of lightning.

Take me, take me I say, you childhood,
take me song of old age, eternal, never to be forgotten,
you great illusion without metaphors,
clumsily opened window, cruel and deep
to all the colors of eternity.

Take me through this rain, path,
return me mild to this small harbor,
this gentle nest of dreams.

III

Horses

Arrive sluggish, arrive weary horses of space,
(the rains pale, mute and pathless)
before the cribs of my hands on the window.

Feed, I say, feed yourself sweating horses
damp with the tepid steam that drenches
from the hips of the night.

Neigh wildly, make me shout too,
alight bird with forgotten wings,
weary mare, goat-legged dancer,
let us leap through this window

together and out of it again
and always without stopping to rest,
over the shadowy clarity of space.

Simic

BALLAD OF TIME

I listen to time dying

Beside the falling leaves
and the frost nipping at hands
how far did I get

Time dies in all that is born
and there is always less and less of me
even if by a step

Autumn is rich in dreams
if sometimes sad
in the receding waters
there is no sailing

The rich November fogs
what do the rivers nurse them with
In their shallow waters
how far shall I get

I listen to time dying

From Autumn in the cold
one fruit is left
that asks with blue lips
where shall I get to

Mihailovich

BRANKO MILJKOVIĆ 1934–61

Branko Miljković was born in 1934 in Niš, Serbia. He graduated from the University of Belgrade and began publishing poetry in 1955. In 1961 he committed suicide, which has created a growing legend around his powerful poetic personality.

His books of poetry are: *Uzalud je budim* (In Vain I Wake Her, 1959), *Smrću protiv smrti* (Death Against Death, 1959), *Poreklo nade* (The Origin of Hope, 1960), *Vatra i ništa* (Fire and Nothing, 1960), and *Krv koja svetli* (The Shining Blood, 1961). He also wrote critical essays and translated the French Symbolists and the Russian poet, Osip Mandelstam.

Influenced by French and Russian Symbolists, as well as by the intellectual Surrealism of Bonnefoy, Miljković's poetry abounds in epigrammatic utterances, unexpected metaphoric constructions, and a philosophical questioning, resulting in a poetry of heightened lyricism. He attained near perfection in form and considerable depth thematically, but in his concern for the role of the poet and poetry, he was eventually led to pessimism and rebelliousness. His influence has been great among the younger poets.

BLACK HORSEMAN

Wild night bitter and vertical
like a fence a black horseman advances
to contrive a plot with roads
night closed tightly into a fist

His voice will empty the audible space
his words will wake nightmares
on the bottom of his black eye lies
a dog ready to bark at any heaven

Black horseman imagined by the bitter
night wild night which the horseman carried
down frightening roads that quarreled
and parted to four corners of the world

Black horseman no one knows
whose name the winds scattered
black horseman the only one to seek us
beyond ourselves and slay our absence

O terrible thought of the black horseman
when in the morning we got up bloody
our throats cut our arms severed
powerless to shout and grasp

O terrible thought of the black horseman
seen for the first time on Red Banii
who imprisoned in our skull
Still gallops from its front to its back

Simic

IN VAIN I WAKE HER

I wake her for the sun self-explained by plants
for the sky strung between fingers
I wake her for words that burn throat
I love her with my ears
You have to go to the world's end and find dew on grass
I wake her for far away things that resemble these
for people who frontless and nameless pass down the street
for anonymous words of city squares I wake her
for the manufactured landscapes of public parks
I wake her for this planet of ours that will perhaps
              be a mine in a bleeding sky
for the smile in stone of comrades asleep between two battles
When the sky was no longer a big bird cage

                    but an aerodrome
my love full of others is part of the dawn
I wake her for the dawn for love for myself for
                                        others
I wake her though this is more vain than calling
                        a bird that alighted forever
she surely said: let him look for me and see I'm
                            not there
this woman with the hands of a child whom I love
this child asleep without having dried her tears that I'm waking
in vain in vain in vain
in vain I wake her
for she will awake different and new
in vain I wake her
for her lips will fail to tell her
in vain I wake her
you know what flows but it does not speak
in vain I wake her
you have to promise a lost name someone's face
                        in the sand

Nejgebauer

MINERS

They descended into hell after injustice
on which it is possible to warm oneself

Simic

AGON

While the river banks are quarreling
The waters flow quietly

Simic

IN PRAISE OF PLANTS

V

I know your root
But what is the grain from which your shadow grows
Vegetal beauty so long invisible
        in the seed
You found under the earth my headless body
        that dreams a true dream
Stars lined up in a pod
All that is created with song and sunlight
Between my absence and your herbal
        ambitions of night
That make me needed even when I'm absent
Green microphone of my subterranean voice
        weed
Growing out of hell since there is no other sun
        under the earth
O plant where are your angels resembling
        insects
And my blood that weaves oxygen and time

Simic

EVERYBODY WILL WRITE POETRY

A dream is an ancient and forgotten truth
which no one can verify now
now the foreign lands sing like sea and troubles
the east is west of the west this false movement is the fastest
now even the birds of my neglected illness sing wisdom
a flower between ashes and fragrance
those who refuse to survive love
and lovers who turn back the time
a garden whose scents the earth doesn't remember
and the earth that remains true to death
for this world is not the sun's only worry

but one day
there where the heart was the sun will stand
and no word tongue can say
will the poem reject
everybody will write poetry
the truth will be there in every word
there where the poem is most beautiful
he who began to sing will withdraw
leaving the singing to others
I announce the great thought of future poetries:
an unhappy man cannot be a poet
I take upon me the verdict of that singing multitude
he who doesn't know how to listen to a poem
     will listen to a storm

but:

will freedom know how to sing
the way the slaves have sung about it

Mihailovich & Wright

SEA WITHOUT POETS

You wait for a moment to adapt yourself to words
But there is no such poet
Nor a word fully free
O bitter and blind sea
In love with shipwreck

Simic

SLEEPERS

Awake I steal what they dream.

Simic

REQUIEM (VIII)

> *Death should be made a holiday because
> the night can take our place any minute*

The Last Prayer for the Dead

For those who have taken advantage boldly
of the possibility to die for those who
have stepped over their own corpses for their
death so necessary against death
for those who are now one
because the world is divided by human skin
into two parts and two and two equals
one when the last night falls
for those who have drowned
in the waters of eternal sleep as the sun
dies at the bottom of a distant landscape
buried for those whose words
have sprouted from the earth like medicine and revolt
let the distant sunflowers bow their heads

Mihailovich

A BALLAD

Wisdom, the day breaks innocently
I no longer have the right for simple words.
My heart is growing dim, my eyes glow.

Sing wonderful old men while over our heads
The stars burst like metaphors.
What disappears above, rots below.
Bird, I will lead you to words but give back
The flame you borrowed. Do not blaspheme the ashes.
In a strange heart we heard our own heart beat
For to sing and to die is the same.

Sun is a word unable to glitter.
Conscience cannot sing because it fears
Its own emptiness. Thieves of visions,
The eagles peck at me from within, I stand
Nailed to a rock that doesn't exist.
With stars we have signed our false bargain
Of invisible night, so much darker. Remember
That fall into life was a proof of your embers.
When ink ripens into blood everyone will know
That to sing and to die is the same.

Wisdom, the stronger one will be the first to give up.
Only a son of a bitch knows what poetry is.
Thieves of fire without compassion,
Tied to the mast of a ship followed
Under water by a song made more dangerous by reality.
The dim sun in the ripe fruit will know how
To replace the kiss that soothes the ashes,
But no one after us will have the strength
To endear himself to a nightingale
When to sing and to die is the same.

Life is fatal but it resists death.
Some terrible pestilence will be named after us.
We've suffered so much. Now the tamed hell
Sings. Let the heart not hesitate
When to sing and to die is the same.

Mihailovich & Simic

BORISLAV RADOVIĆ 1935–

Born in 1935 in Belgrade, where he studied world literature at the University of Belgrade, Borislav Radović has been a professional writer ever since.

He writes poetry and essays, and translates from French. His books of poetry include: *Poetičnosti* (Poeticalness, 1956), *Ostale poetičnosti* (Other Poeticalness, 1959), *Maina* (1964), *Bratstvo po nesanici* (Brotherhood in Insomnia, 1967), and *Opisi, gesla* (Descriptions, Slogans, 1970).

Radović strives for a synthesis of a rationalistic, meditative poise and subtle sensitivity and emotion. His verse is melodic and playful, although beneath the peaceful surface one can sense conflict and tension. He is skilful and articulate, utilizing the linguistic possibilities as one of his main tools. Radović is one of the leading members of the middle generation in contemporary Serbian poetry.

from THE LIVING RIVER

I

In the beginning, this was the purest imprint, the impending nearness. How mad that clarity was. Pellicle, ready to initiate the moment, to begin contact beyond the point. Where you dawn I fall like stone. I yield to your law: to be lowered beneath each memory. To flow into someone's sleeplessness, to darken her terror with all my medicinal faces. Ice took her.

And here all mild gestures sum themselves; the gradual slanted movements. I speak, so that you may flow

★

How to reach the moral of the text, to rip oneself into the depths and penetrate headless? Our wedding will be

vertical: to gather you up, for you to make me sink. The
frog-heaven winks from below. Still lower, there are
crushed petals, soft lime ribs, and still lower the lost
warmth. And solution, barely visible, of lazy and simmering
mists. All the dregs of your scholarship and plunder.

*

I was the voice of thirst calling a long time
Into the reality of this innocent orgy.

I was and saw where irrefutable you grow
Above the horizon of hope and branches.

Once I saw your jugular vein
Beyond aging and beyond dying.

I was the dry consciousness that dreams you awake.

*

You are my foreboding of fierce speech from sleeping lips:
rage or its solitary flowing essence. It widens the capacity
of your soul. Everything within you is thicker, denser,
more somber and more essential. Everything within you is
far deeper and still I permeate you as though I dream of
you.

From above, your ceaseless vowels renew the primeval shapeless
lucidity, the sacredness of our relationship. I thaw before
you liquid silence. I listen whether you exist. In your
kernel, the shivers come to life again. I understand you,
as though I drink you.

II

I speak while you teach me the accent lost since the
ancient ancestors, you return me to the era of the lip,
teach me universality of touch and yoke, the indivisible
lust. There is no perfidy or pity between us. You let
me be immersed in the blue yeast, where busy with your

rashness, weary of your monstrous experience, I become
that which I breathe.

III

You tease, I accept. I make you a sister, dark and humble,
submissive. The returning skies are low above us. The
image cannot be dissolved. Your braided constellations
seek me out and give me direction; the strokes grow
lighter. Instead of any effort, I leave my blackness
within you. Here we are a single wound, a single blade.

★

Wounded by clarity. Crushed by freshness.
Although I am still able to deny.
Wounded by freshness. Aren't they cold
The hands on the true bottom of your heart?

Although I am still able to forgive,
To resist and to give in,
I am nothing but that bottom I await,

Nothing but the joy of the deepest fall.

IV

I speak to postpone recognition, to make you doubt,
muddle you up; to conceal your true nature. I speak
to seduce you. I speak to make you equal to the words
which you don't admit, which you don't even distinguish.

★

First I call you kernel: to attack you, to free you.
Then, within you, I am the model of a husk of everything
that ripens beyond. To express you, the idea of the
shirt is not necessary; and we are closer than that.
There is no depth that can take you away from me any
longer. Who thinks of you, dissolves in your laziness,
alive with impatience. I do not stir, the end approaches.

I am in your pupil when my sight is keen. Who drowns
in you, sees through you.

Simic

A FOREST

We found no way to struggle with death.
We found no road in you, old forest,
To your great clearing, where we had left
Our calipers and angry lovers.
It all happened between two showers and two lightnings.
And now we are here, with moss and books;
A forgotten noon.
From the pine tower a woodpecker pecks
The alphabet of a wild dying. There is no sky,
Nor deep soil fattened by the roots;
Only the air expands
And forks into darting tongues everywhere
Into the green fate of a song,
To preserve us until the axes arrive,
Open a tree and calm down the world.

Mihailovich

WHITENESS

A word is a drawing of the long suffering of speech,
The sign of joy on the forehead of mute caves;

Emptiness is white: as old as thought,
Precise as a distant window in the evening.

A knee dancing around a fire and a mound.

Mihailovich

NAKEDNESS

Here no one builds, you take the round-about way
By the curve of some enormous thigh,
By the cruel tooth of some threatening breast,
By the rugged side of the heart.

There were not even voices in the blue.
Only the snow kept falling or feathers;
Memory of slain birds,
Powerless cold mountain-ridge.

Then we came and transplanted
Great nakedness, before which rustle
Only the superfluous leaves.

Mihailovich & Simic

from THE PRIMEVAL BOND

VI

Were we playing, and what kind of game,
Or did we lose our way
In a common distant whirlpool
Where we sought for a new tongue:

No one knows that, now others seek us

In the spur of a ditch and among rocks
Of taciturn tooth-keen hills,
In places unusual for love:
Others, who will be silent about us;

But did they ever exist
Those signs of ours, incestuous pictures,

Or did we only live speechless
In our mute tale
With an infallible sun in the nape;
You with gods, I with a stone plough,
Like two severed sentences,

No one will know that.

Mihailovich

GLORY TO EROS

The mist will be your visage and a sigh your name,
Bright wings in a cocoon that covers silken consciousness
In the heart of the moment, while thought still lives
And body is lost, leaving no droplet, imponderable.

In a glass house, your heart's lightning
Shall beat out luxuriant time, the measure of the poem's age.
Often, through narrow windows, one will see
You pacing up and down, measuring nothing.

Your world will be the lone one of imagination
Where the eye sees what eye is not to see.
There you will seek an everlasting place for lying words,
For noble words that have no meaning.

You, shadow, will speak, will read, will spit,
Contender with our mother, Nature; a possibility, a law.
The poem, you will hear only in death
Reveal itself in still unwritten signs.

Champe

BOŽIDAR TIMOTIJEVIĆ 1932–

Born in Rakovica near Belgrade, Bozidar Timotijević
studied world and Yugoslav literature at the University
of Belgrade, and serves as an editor with literary journals
and publishing houses.

He has published the following books of poetry: *Veliki
spavač* (The Great Sleeper, 1958), *Srebrno brdo* (A Silvery
Hill, 1959), *Slovo ljubve* (A Word of Love, 1960), *Dan se
radja* (The Day Is Breaking, 1963), *Večernje* (Vespers,
1966), and *Aždajkinje* (She-Dragons, 1970).

Both traditional and modern, Timotijević has always
stressed the purely lyrical quality and immediacy of his
expression. Most of his poems are intimate, somewhat
melancholy, and always highly melodic.

TWO CRYSTAL GLASSES

I have seen (and then perhaps not) all things:
they spoke their language of migrants.
But: two beautiful crystal glasses stood
one afternoon on the edge of a table and observed
the world unfolding before them and before itself.
That was the moment. And those two beautiful etc.
glasses on the edge of a roughly-hewn table
bothered no one and were a thorn in nobody's flesh,
they were even consistently good and silent, at night
as well as during the day, and served with their mute beings
man's passion, as every other invention.
But: two beautiful etc. glasses which stood
one afternoon on the edge of a you-know-what table,
were grabbed by the diligent proletarian hand of a man
who knew metals as he knew his own wife, and
he poured into them his soul with the full force
of his worker's and warrior's heart—he grabbed
the two beautiful crystal glasses and with a gesture which
told of a destroyed personal happiness, slammed those two

mute glasses on the concrete floor and then formally
paid their crystal value in cash
and went home in clear conscience like an ant.

Two crystal glasses of that afternoon now lie
on a well-known garbage dump by the river and no longer
   speak
the language of migrants, and I, who saw all that,
know only one thing—and I was told that by the same man
who so lightheartedly took away their crystalness and mind—
he said: "They belong in the bowels of the earth
   just like hell."

Mihailovich

from THE TRUTH OF BLACK THINGS

I

Sometimes the truth of black things gathers above me
its mournful power never to forget anything.

Then I leave my bricklayer's trade and pay a visit
to those familiar regions flocking above my forehead.

Over all maps the birds do not stir. Men struggle through
fantastic landscapes. Warfare of dogs and moonlight. Mad trees

have made a circle with silence and all is now a faultless
mummy. If only this instant would come to its end,

I too would start to call myself a mummy. But the gods
are kind. When we give them human power they keep quiet.

With us, though, things are different. Sometimes the truth
of black things descends on me and I wish to burn once again.

II

In the world of black things I inhabited my blind silence
resembling bugs, shivering disembodied,

lowering my head into the lap of mild winds.
That visit that made memories from the pit of my palm,

understood the threads of my disappearance. Sadly they ran
through my blood the beautiful ghosts of my days, inventing

illusion as an innocent game. A small snake
which resembles emptiness had gnawed its wound

through the marrows of my heart. I came to know the kingdom
in my body from its cornerstone, the livid darkness of words

in the evil of the world. In the world of black things
I am nibbling now my silence to make it beautiful,

to stop it from setting in the back of my house, toward
my gentle grave. In the world of black things as you see

I found my truth. Now I am waiting for Summer.

Simic

WATERS

Somewhere under the window and the bed
waters reigned.
Ugly waters dirtied by death
flowed through our ears.

We stood half-naked on the hill—
suddenly a beautiful sight:
a wave like tar, a dragon of foam
leaped over a child's belly.

Mihailovich

HAND

Dead are the windows of this house
which merges with the lake in the distance.
The door has fallen silent and now only
the dry wind of summer sleeps in there.

And secretly brings in a white hand,
a hand that offers no resistance,
but what is it doing with her there
at this hour of unconscious darkness?

How does her tenderness behave
in the empty rooms covered with spiderwebs only,
didn't she find a way to escape
and take a bath in the lake once again?

Mihailovich

LJUBOMIR SIMOVIĆ 1935–

Ljubomir Simović was born in 1935 in Titovo Užice, Serbia. He studied Yugoslav literature at the University of Belgrade, and is now a program editor at the Belgrade radio-television station.

His poetic output is relatively small: *Slovenske elegije* (Slavic Elegies, 1958), *Veseli grobovi* (Gay Tombs, 1961), *Poslednja zemlja* (The Last Land, 1964), *Šlemovi* (Helmets, 1967), and *Uoči trećih petlova* (Before the Third Rooster Crow, 1972). Several of his poems were published in the United States in *Four Yugoslav Poets*.

From his early romantic and youthful exuberance, Simović has slowly changed into a somber poet of protest against war and the dehumanization of modern existence. His poems combine a simplicity of language with an expressionistic imagery, and a kind of Breughelian earthiness. He has mastered form, avoiding excesses and unnecessarily complex expression. His verse is traditional, simple, and concrete, his strongest tool being metaphor. The main goal of his engagement as an artist is the return to humanism and sensibility.

EPITAPHS FROM KARANSKO CEMETERY

Here rest Tiosav
son of Miljka and Stamena
evening wind circles the candle
chases its shadow around it
the wheat has grown to the stars
the evening descends between tombs
here rests Tiosav buried with his shepherd's flute
here rests dead
Tiosav who wanted to live even
turned into a frog forgive Lord even
turned into a green tree

Refrain

    oi cloudy wind flies up into mist of warm swamps
    a single ancient star is creating all this confusion
    oi stop saying no to this bird falling down
    into sun–lit flame into head of King Lazarus

Stanoje two months old
sleeps in a cradle of soil
nobody remembers him
born at the end of Autumn died at the beginning of Winter
darling among the dead
neither friends nor enemies remember him
his weeping cannot be told
his mound cannot be jumped over or avoided
his mound slowly turns into a dirt road
in a small hell of lit candles
over his grave it is dark

    Refrain

    oi cold wind flies up into mist of warm swamps
    a single ancient star is creating all this confusion
    see the bird falling down from this scented sky
    into sunlit flame into skull of King Lazarus

Koviljka daughter of Milisav and Stojanka
lived sixteen years
died on Ivan's day
wreaths of birds break open in the sky
a mongrel loiters around the grave covered with flowers
a young man and a girl sleep naked on a hill
scented by the air of pine trees but the cross
spreads its arms and won't let us go further
neither into forest nor
into river nor into
the air

Refrain

oi blue wind flies up into mist of warm swamps
this starry morning is creating all this confusion
oi stop scream no to this bird falling down
into sunlit flame into tomb of King Lazarus

Dirge

Lit candles like spears
Stuck, oi, into smoking
Furrows. Over the body of hemp,
Air deep to the morning star.
Above my head wax candles rustle
On my coffin apples tumble.

Simic

NOTATION IN GOLD

Among bloody candles I welcomed winter 1254.
Every night, to the chorus of wolves and blizzards,
my vigil lasted as long as the path of the flame
from top to bottom of the candle, when with crow's
feather I wrote the pages of monastic chronicles
for the year 1235 of our Lord.

In this small cell
I recognize summer by dust, winter by snow dust
sifted through narrow cracks.

The candle above my blinded eyes, knotted
like a finger of a leper with sharp nails of its flame,
already for many years points to heaven and reminds me.

Over my head, the bells sway

large like golden haystacks,
once long ago in the village of Volujci.

I dream I do not exist, I dream that someone
dreams of me and that the dawn is approaching,
and that the time is coming for him to awake.

Simic

EPITAPH

To the chimney a bull's horns
To the window a lamb's skin
To the tomb a raven's feathers
To the kettle a cloud and smoke
To the hearth a bit of grass
To the Autumn rain and stars
To the cloud a King's galleon
And to me through the Autumn air
Over my only fire
A shovel full of black earth.

Simic

ONE EVENING

I was a belfry and blizzard of birds,
and ramparts, and the chalice thrown from the ramparts;
     now it's in the sea and the sea is in it;
I was King cleaning the boots of the bootmaker,
I was pigeon on a marble helmet,
a square and the ropemaker weaving the rope
and the criminal hung by that rope.

I was soldier raising his glass like a flag
and another, in the stable,

on top of a nurse who embraces him fainting.
In the grass, with flowers high to horse's belly,
I was the horse and its rider, night through which they ride,
I was the fields, the messenger and his evil tidings.

I was everywhere and everyone, seeking how to throw off my back
these worries and animals, violence of fear and flowers,
evil and inclination to evil:
                                but early one sleepless
evening, before a storm, in western Serbia, I saw
great flight of birds which as they rose from a tree
made it seem as if the tree had disappeared.

Simic

TRAVELING STAR

I

Is anyone waiting for you at the end of the road?
Is the sky empty without man?

Or are you dark because you know
Of an even darker sun on which it's Winter?

The gloom of the day that will not come
And how much ash remains from a single sun?

II

Is your glitter your speech? Did you shine
When they hung you by the tongue?

When my head fell in the mud,
You sent me greetings from heavenly gallows?

And while the executioner wove the rope,
What is it that I understood in your glow

So I keep silent before men that offer me bread,
And before judges ready to forgive me.

Simic

VENO TAUFER 1933–

Veno Taufer was born in Ljubljana in 1933. He graduated in history and theory of literature at the University of Ljubljana, was a TV reporter and radio announcer, and now is a free-lance writer. He has written poetry and essays and has translated from several languages, mostly English. His books of poetry include *Svinčene zvezde* (Lead Stars, 1958), *Jetnik prostosti* (The Prisoner of Freedom, 1963), and *Vaje in naloge* (Examples and Exercises, 1969). He has also written a verse play, *Prometej ali tema v zenici sonca* (Prometheus or The Dark in the Sun's Pupil, 1968).

As a member of the "Perspective" group, Taufer actively sought to bring Slovenian poetry into the mainstream of contemporary European poetry. Influenced mostly by modern English poetry, his work exhibits neo-expressionist and surrealist traits. Like many of his contemporaries in Slovenian poetry, he too is concerned with the problems and dilemmas of modern life, with rebellion and negation of reality. A philosophy of fear and the absurd permeates most of his poems.

OPEN-AIR CONCERT

she with tin legs
hourglass in mouth aquarium in her head
he with all the town's staircases on his back
under his arm a heart that can be wound up or stopped

they open a book and look for a road
to water sky and blossoming grove
where there's no sweating paper no fumbling eyes
where like in a B picture pretty birds twitter

she opens her legs unlocks the aquarium
starts hunting for fish

he climbs the stairs and winds up his heart

nude bodies drown in sand from the hourglass
fish flick through their veins
with dark designs concealed in their bloody gills

Taufer & Scammell

DEPARTURE

I
The ship shuffles at the fat mole
a bashful clown
in a brashly lit circus tent

The sailors are in the pub
spinning black and green yarns
and captains adventures to porcelain women

The word has become
bitter fruit
on bloody lips

A sailor steps from the pub
slaps the tight bottom of the night
swallows the moon and spits it into the sea

He hollows his body
points the plated white prow in his eyes
at the departing flocks of sea and sky

The living flesh absorbs firmly
the steel mast
the scabs of pain on it crack
blood
        drenches the sail.

II

The wind's rickety limbs
have sprouted moldy fungus

The rancid meat of fantasy
has disintegrated

We have laid the grey bones
to rest

We are leaving on tiptoe we are leaving
through gates of scaly silence

Why should we cry among monuments
that stink of rotten rain

We will return to the bones
which will be white from their sleep

We will put on an act
greet them like new friends

But they will recognize us and know
that we cried because of them

Moldy fungus has sprouted
on the wind's rickety limbs
it can barely hobble among us

Taufer & Scammell

HAMLET 69

each night is a slipping under the surface
listening to the rain as it rots the pile of papers
until in the cup of the morning eternity passes
the sun rises flicks out the razor

your face is wakened by a sliver of metal
you sense the feel of your vein beating
eye hears hand tongue touches time
you rejoice at the life of the razor

your image is mirrored in it
and the world neatly round it
closer to the world's center you spin

whole worlds on the narrow blade with you
suddenly potent to destroy
what destroying is destroyed

Taufer & Scammell

COMPUTER SONNET WITH INTRODUCTION AND COMMENTARY

one: introduction (dream)

into a skull containing 10,000 million brain cells was
inserted one of the latest types of computer, comprising
somewhat over 50,000 cells accommodated in a large hall

two: sonnet

out of the sod flickers moses like the finger of god
lovers like the guests of god lie down on the earth in
the dense rays all over the earth the word locks them up
with inaudible keys by the codes on their skin

then the learning by heart begins
till the lover can reckon the flame
the fire's not forgotten till the beloved knows the sum
of her issue she doesn't forget she gave birth

until the fruit knows all the bonfires of history

from cain to the plate on the family table
until moses breaks his tables

until the word knows by heart it's forgotten
and forgotten death that it's not locked in at all
and the son finds the red sea empty

three: commentary

I tell you truly
I like you so badly
I like you so badly
I tell you truly

I'd bear you as many children
as fish in the sea in the night
as birds in the sky in the day
I'd bear you as many children

without you I'd feel so badly
fishes would swim in the tears
birds would fly on the sighs
without you I'd feel so badly

Taufer & Scammell

DANE ZAJC 1929–

Born in Zgornja Javorščica, Slovenia, Dane Zajc is a librarian. He has published three books of poetry: *Požgana trava* (Burned Grass, 1958), *Jezik iz zemlje* (A Tongue from the Earth, 1961), and *Ubijavci kač* (The Snake Killers, 1969). He has also written a verse-play, *Otroci reke* (Children of the River, 1962).

Zajc's small output belies the magnitude of his poetic qualities. As a member of the middle generation of contemporary Slovenian poets, he shares with others the concern for man's loneliness and alienation, his inability to escape fear, horror, and the awareness of the futility of existence. Zajc's poems are pregnant with philosophical implications, expressed in simple but beautiful form, although they are difficult to penetrate at times because of their hermetic quality.

from GOTHIC WINDOWS

II

At night the rubies commence to glow
on your breasts, Magdalena.
Two red rubies under your veil.
In the gloom of the cathedral.
In the white smoke of snuffed candles.
Throw off your veil.

Throw it off: the dry rustle of sin
in the odor of prayers.
With a dry smack the stars will fall
from your head.
In the bright stream the stars will pour
from your eyes into my open mouth.
The rubies of your body
will drop into my lap.
The moon will be licking your lips

with its red tongue of passion.

Throw off your veil, Magdalena.
Tomorrow you will stand in the spraying light of the sun
naked. Humiliated.
Mine.

Taufer & Scammell

LUMP OF ASH

For a long time you carry fire in your mouth.
For a long time you hide it.
Behind a bony fence of teeth.
Squeezing within the magic circle of your lips.
You know that no one must sniff
the smoke from your mouth.
You remember that crows kill the white crow.
Therefore you lock up your mouth.
And hide the key.

But one day you feel the word in your mouth.
It fills the cave of your head with echoes.

Then you start to look for the key of your mouth.
For a long time you look.
When you find it you unlock the lichen of your lips.
You unlock the rust of your teeth.
Then you look for a tongue.
But there is no tongue.
Then you want to utter the word.
But your mouth is full of ash.
And instead of the word a lump of ash
stirs in the soot
of your throat.

Then you discard the rusty key.

Then you make yourself a new tongue of earth.
A tongue that speaks words of soil.

Taufer & Scammell

THE GARDEN

He came back shriveled.
Only the furrow behind him in the yellow sand
showed that he was moving.

From their perches the lookouts reported:
something is coming out of the desert.
They gathered on the border.
They pulled him into the world of green.
I am the one you sent, he said.
It was like pincers talking
when he spoke.

Then his head slumped down,
impaled on a willow wand.
He's not one of us, they thought,
and gazed at his doggish tongue
licking the grass.

What news from the Forbidden, they asked.
It's all true, he shivered,
and the pincers of his mouth closed shut.

They dropped water onto his tongue and demanded:
Isn't there a garden on the other side?
Isn't everything we don't have in that garden?
Everything you know is true, he rustled.

This isn't the one we sent, they said,
and slit his vein.
Then the slow grey liquid came oozing out of it,
they were sure
he was a hostile being.
They left him there. (His ribs thinned to
sticks of brushwood.)
They chose a new messenger.

Taufer & Scammell

SOWER-HEAD

On the nonroad along which the steps pitter-pattered
the pain on the head's western continent said:
I've been building this hive for ages
and filling it with honey which you don't taste,
which is alien to you,
which you won't drink because I am filtering it
out of your flesh.

In the place called now, later or always the steps come
    to a halt,
because the foot said:
I am sick of my name.
It will be no use rolling it round your tongue any more.

Nobody saw the head that rolled down the slope
with a mask of earth and stuck with bandaids of decay:
I am coming back forever. I am coming back to freedom,
    it sang,
drunkenly scattering teeth
and happily losing eyes in the wet grass.
It rolled to a halt in a ravine
and crouched
and took a long time wasting to perfection.

182 •

From here it is impossible to see anywhere.
Nowhere do we find the one who was robbed,
who scattered.
To think of him is harder
than to think of the hole after the tòoth is gone.

Scammell

GREGOR STRNIŠA 1930–

A native of Ljubljana, where he studied German at the university, Gregor Strniša later became a free-lance writer.

So far he has published five books of verse: *Mozaiki* (Mosaics, 1959), *Odisej* (Odysseus, 1963), *Zvezde (Stars, 1965)*, *Samorog* (Unicorn, 1966), and *Brobdingnag* (1968). He has also written a number of plays.

Strniša is one of the best among the younger Slovenian poets. He is a unique and highly articulate poet, whose confessional reactions to fear and alienation are expressed through elaborate historical allegories, striking metaphors, and dream sequences. While he frequently employs old motifs and myths, he also epitomizes the increasing concern of the contemporary Slovenian poets with the perennial problems of meaning and existence.

EVENING FAIRYTALE

Trees open their trunks with a dry crack
and the dark hearts hidden within
start to beat with the wound of distant drums.
Grey mosses hang from the yellow moon.

Then great stones stand up,
walk around on spindly legs,
like huge grey spiders,
and gnaw the soft faces of mushrooms.

On the wood's far side, in a dark house,
in the deep low pits of their rooms,
people are sleeping like long grey mice,
teased by the big cats of dreams.

Strniša

A SHIP

On a long, long trail, a dark ship.
On the masts the silvery jewelry of the moon,
southern winds leaning against the large sails,
showers pour along the grey path of the sea.

The sailors' eyes burn like coal from thirst.
The fiery captain seeks the way in darkness.
The sun hewn from heavy gold
and the seven stars of Orion shine above the ship.

High up on the masts the flags
flutter gaily like apparitions.
With the stern wrapped up in sea grass,
the depth glides like a cloud, like a star
        over the creatures that are rigid.

Mihailovich

from BROBDINGNAG

III
The glowing fires of Brobdingnag
under a red-eyed moon.
In the smithies the ring of steel,
the smoke rises to the white heights.

In Brobdingnag they have cast
a bell that echoes the world's heart.
It hangs in the snowbound valley
But there is no man there.

The murmuring reaches from the bell,
And as the bell's bronze sings softly,
the glowing dream in the world's heart
remembers the primeval sun.

V

The unknown people of Brobdingnag
three-eyed, with three heads,
and a god, huge and black as the earth,
with a name a thousand days long.

In the magic land—the story goes—
five valleys converge somewhere
and there, between five mountains,
Brobdingnag has its heart.

Is the lake there perhaps blue
or the glacier green perhaps?
About Lilliput everything is known
but about Brobdingnag nothing ever.

Mihailovich

from CRO-MAGNON

I

Death arrives quietly, quickly
with rustling steps.
We saw the striped tiger
heavy with fruit in the grass.

Just above our heads
through the blue vault of the cave,
white ghosts drift,
the golden bug crawls and disappears.

We heard the bird of bright feathers,
the laughter of an unknown beast in the night,
death arrives quietly, quickly
with rustling steps.

III

Perhaps we have called these things
by their names;
those who come after us
will understand better.

The wind that frightens the trees,
the forest of death, the starry fish,
the insect that flies through the red dusk of Spring,
the white snow, the dark mountain.

The heavy track of the beast is in the earth.
That one we'll never get to know.
Those who come after us
will find some name for her too.

V

Bad dreams rule the tribe
hidden in the cave of the highest mountain.
Above them like clothes in tatters
illness, storms, and death.

Thus we live in the great ditch.
Something glitters in the blue vault,
the golden bug with numerous feet,
the grey and smoking pillar of the volcano.

In the great hole where we live
we gave names to things.
Now death arrives quietly, quickly,
the running wind frightens the trees.

Simic

HELMETS

I

It happened in the city that doesn't exist,
in a land that is no more.
They arrived from all sides.
Early frost drifted down from the hills.

They stood in a circle, one more circle.
Some have sailed here in ships,
and some have already traveled
many months.

Night was falling. The feast of helmets
in late Autumn.
High in the hills the virgin of heaven
walked the difficult paths.

II

All night before the feast he didn't sleep.
He remembered the long road.
With the gold ring in his hand
he sometimes touched his eyes.

They stood in a circle, one more circle.
The golden fire burned in the middle,
fire that thaws down the night
as the wind thaws the touch of southern winds.

A man stepped forward from the circle,
stood in the light and returned among the shadows.
He didn't know himself. As in a dream
he stepped forward and opened his hand.

III

It happened in the city that doesn't exist,
in a land that is no more.
They sung with words
ancient as time:

We stand in a circle, one more circle.
The world of shadows is all around us.
Above is the sky, impenetrable,
black and without stars.

To the fire that thaws down the night
as it thaws the touch of southern winds,
we give rings from our left hands,
the jewels from our breasts.

V

From the mountain saddle he looked back.
The feather of smoke rose above the roofs.
Like a wreath of sooty helmets
the houses spread below him.

He heard the quiet rustle of snowflakes
from the invisible sky.
The city floated like an apparition
over the deaf whiteness of snow.

Like a wreath of ashes in the arms of the world
that was silent and white,
then the thick curtain of snow
slowly hid the city from his eyes.

Simic

ODYSSEUS

V

In the windy nights the spring comes and goes.
Behind him are unruly flocks of multi-colored birds,
in the waves before him lies a black cliff,
covered with heavy, wrinkled sea shells.

On a narrow shore dividing birds and shells
he sits between the land of shells and the land of birds.
Every evening when the sun touches the sea
a shell opens and quietly glides to the sea bottom.

He sits on the shore with a clump of earth in his fingers,
above the frothy wave of the dark sea.
The sea is heavy with shells and dead ships.
The winter comes and goes, the spring goes and returns.

Mihailovich

AUTUMN

Low huts of rain are standing
on autumn's empty shore.
Deer-people with grey hearts
are asleep on the beach. A mist rises.

From out of their foreheads, like dreams,
grow heavy antlers
and sometimes, as in sleep, a man rises
and stands at the edge of the water.

Spring is remote, like a green stone
in the heart of the black windy mountain.

In the evening the moon begins to swell and swell,
veils the world with a red shadow.
A deer-man walks through the red dusk,
along the grey edge of the water.

Scammell

THE PRIESTS

When we burn out the heart,
not a single drop flows.
When we burn out the whole heart,
a small black mask remains.

The mask has the likeness of God
or resembles the devil.
More often than God's face
we see the devil's.

A river flows down the snowy mountain.
In the cave a mute flame gutters.
With its help we have changed man
into a shriveled black effigy of the devil.

Scammell

THE GRAVES

Through little lands two horses drew
a clay effigy of the dead king.
Clay horses beneath a clay moon.
The little years passed quickly.

A clay maiden in the cart
played fast songs on a silent zither.
Now and then a long wave rocked the ship
far out to sea of the departing potter.

Ship of oak foreseen in a green acorn,
apparition of light on the sword's tip—
tiny country made out of clay
in the big black country of earth.

Scammell

DUBRAVKO HORVATIĆ 1939–

Dubravko Horvatić was born in Zagreb, where he studied comparative literature and art history at the University of Zagreb, and where he now lives as a free-lance writer.

He writes poetry, literature for juveniles, and literary and art criticism. His collections of poems include *Groznica* (Fever, 1960), *Zla vojna* (Evil Battle, 1963), *Bedem* (Wall, 1968), and *Crna zemlja* (Black Earth, 1970).

In his early poetry, Horvatić raised his protest against the inhumanity and horror of war. In later poems he has turned to some of the perennial questions, expressing fear and doubt in the meaning of existence, and generally striking more pessimistic tones.

* * *

From generation to generation we besiege this city, storm the same walls, curse the same towers, and from generation to generation build fires, dig tunnels, climb these fortifications, from generation to generation break our spears and heavy devices against the walls. There were those, the old songs say, who were already on the towers, but they tumbled back, before other warriors' feet, as if struck by lightning. For a thousand years the city has been invincible, the walls stand even though no one is defending them. Now we the innocents storm them, inheriting a pledge to raise the flag on the main tower, we storm during the heat and frost, but the walls stand mighty and sturdy, the walls stand as they did a thousand years ago. We attack, but each blasphemes in his heart: is there a city behind the walls at all?

Mihailovich & Moran

* * *

And when finally the embittered armies collide, the hatreds that from time immemorial prepare them for this encounter, for a horrible slaughter and not for an insignificant clash, and when spears and flags, the thunder of the hoofs and the wailing from the broken throats get all intermingled, when the decisive battle finally begins, I will be seen standing on the highest tower defending the city I had built with effort, I will be seen storming with destructive machinery, attacking the wall that stands in my way, and it will be seen how in wrath I aim at myself before the city, how in anger I aim at myself on the tower and how I perish from my own gun, by my own hand in the fiercest battle, I before the city and on the walls of the city, never finding out the outcome of the battle, never experiencing its end.

Mihailovich & Moran

YOU WHO SPOKE ABOUT SAILING

You who spoke about sailing but waded in the muddy water only up to the knees, you who spoke of tenderness while a snake crawled through your shattered bowels, you who called a festering wound a growth on your finger, a topaz, you are not the last of your kind. You are the first. You who now live in ravines and feed on dead dogs, you are our ancestor: for every dawn brings us closer to your homeland. We shall come one day to your kingdom, believing in nothing and only in nothing, we shall come like withered hordes to live as you do. And all that we now hate we shall consider the gift of heaven. There will be only the earth, desolate and turned up, only a few yellow puddles from which we shall greedily slurp, and that sky which will be drenched and which will rot for a long time.

Mihailovich

DANIJEL DRAGOJEVIĆ 1934–

Born in 1934 in Vela Luka, Dalmatia, Danijel Dragojević studied art history at the University of Zagreb and became one of the leading art critics. He now lives as a professional writer.

His first poetry appeared in 1956, and he has published: *Kornjača i drugi predjeli* (A Turtle and Other Landscapes, 1961), *U tvom stvarnom tijelu* (In Your Real Body, 1964), *Svjetiljka i spavač* (Lantern and a Sleeper, 1965), *Nevrijeme i drugo* (Bad Weather and the Rest, 1968), and *Četvrta životinja* (The Fourth Animal, 1972). He also writes art monographs and literary essays.

Dragojević began his career writing poems in prose rich in images. He now writes verse with the emphasis on the philosophical and religious aspects of human life and relationships. The directness and intimacy of his images undoubtedly stem from his knowledge of, and love for, the visual arts.

THE AUTUMN IN WHICH THE SOWERS
DO NOT RECOGNIZE THE NATURE OF THEIR GRAINS

Do you see that the motion by which you governed thousands
                                has withered?
There it is in the caller of a vehicle on an outing,
There it is in your room at the piano.
And how easily we were leaving the home!
Darkness has welcomed us hostilely,
But we, smiling and gay, were not bothered.
The first morning already the dull fall of a body was heard.
Then silence. Later it multiplied, multiplied.
Whether it was betrayal, origin or defense.
Leaning against the wall is a glorious thing.
The road into desired freedom thus began.
Now you part your hair almost casually in the morning.
Neither those sending nor receiving the reports

Were able to read in them the vision of change
That will stand in our nuptial bed like a hairy shadow.
With hatred we answered hatred, suffering with longer suffering,
And now our children wear the faces of the assassinated.

Mihailovich & Moran

FISHING FROM AN OLD PICTURE

Now God's thought is
Among the people pulling the net
Peaceful, beyond the shipwreck,
Beyond the murky sun
That walks around us.

A rare luxury.
A hand—the sign of brotherhood,
Strength grows into action,
A black letter into piety.

Is this a memory
Or a foreboding of the future?

From everywhere, on the open sea
Among these faces,
In the color and in the hands,
In the wet hills behind
Something is telling us,
That perhaps every thing
Could turn good,
The thought as well as the action,
So that we could
Live plainly.

Talk plainly
And with little hope,

Take our bread
From the bottom of sadness.

Mihailovich

THE BACK OF THE DEVIL

What do the dead warriors think today,
When after such a long time, and older,
They recall the days inundated with the smell of bodies,
The smoke and the sin of killing?
The future, their future has been here for some time already,
                      not the one of monuments,
It walks the streets, works and sleeps at night,
Coughs, hiccups, laughs at a road in the back,
It is more learned and shrewder than
It could be thought at the youthful time of marching songs.
In front where they happened
Stands a bronze head and rushes a hundred kilometers per hour
Carrying food, journals and good sleep.
Now they, with their first grey hairs,
Probably wear on their belts some other appendages
And carry on different conversation in the evening
When everything calms down and the time comes for small
                              intimacies.

Mihailovich

THE GRASS

When you enter the grass I do not see you, but
by the swaying of the grass I follow your walk
and know that you will soon fly out at the other
end like a quail.

Mihailovich

UNDER AN UMBRELLA

Perhaps we ought to know better than to come out.
In the immediate dark, deafening thunder, wet feet,
A desire for the warmth of home,
Thinking we are too weak and mortal
Under the large drops.
We could wait a while.
Others sleep peacefully, we
Press round the wooden cane,
The only hard spot at which our room breaks in pieces.
We were never closer than now
When this black rag defends us from the sky.
Never so simple and intimate.
Two naked branches in the night.
Now where are the wishes to build, where is the pride,
The solemn gesture, the rapture of the body?
Perhaps somewhere in a furrow the seed germinates
And in the bright window there are good thoughts
For us after death,
But the water is robbing us of soil,
Preventing our glances from rising,
And everything is wet, charged with emptiness
In the two lost bodies.
Somewhere a dog gnaws a lone bone,
While the lover strains to create a mirror
Among the scattered floor rags.
No despair here, nor a feeling for the future,
One picture and one thought against which we lean—
There is no such dust now.
Everything is so genuine and simple!
It rains, the holes are filling, darkness full of wind.
We slowly trudge away.

Mihailovich & Moran

RADOVAN PAVLOVSKI 1937–

Radovan Pavlovski was born in 1937 in Niš into a Macedonian family. His books of poetry—*Suša, svadba i selidba* (Drought, Wedding, and Moving, 1961), *Suša* (Drought, 1963), *Korabija* (Boat, 1964), *Visoko pladne* (High Noon, 1966), and a book of longer poems, *Niz prozirkata na mečot* (Through the Crack in the Sword, 1971)—have made him one of the leading poets in contemporary Macedonian poetry and one of its strongest talents.

A master of metaphor and poetic image, Pavlovski attempts to combine reality with dream, the here and now with an imaginary land of his own. He is preoccupied with myths, both historical and those created by himself. His capacity for strong imagistic invention combined with an almost animistic approach to the natural world, make his images seem to rise out of the unconsious with the echoes of rural life and folklore.

A YOUNG MAN WHO SLEEPS AT NOON

The sound of death
lulls you to sleep
Wake up
young man
You have a field resonant with plants and hoes
The morning sun is a large feast table
On which the ploughmen break their bread
The noon hides the black threads of night
You have buried rocks and moonlight under your body
Ten horsemen from an ambush
Fly in like the waves of fear
A tender plant ties your fingers to the soil and won't let
you go until you give it
a dimmed kiss at high noon
A choir of dead lovers rises from the grass

Wake up young man
My ship built of grapevine
is at sea with its hoarse throat
There are moments when everything is dead with sleep
There are moments when I study myself to see if I'm mad
It is evening
many people are coming to wake you
You draw a map of stars
and breathe deeply
O wake up young man
and tell us your dreams
On a beautiful horse we shall ride to the Iron River
for the wind from the mills to refresh us
With a wounded flower I button my shirt because of the wind
and enter the house o love

Tell me what drinks do you drink in the dream
that you are not waking up o young man

Mihailovich & Simic

TWO ROOSTERS: RED AND BLACK

A red and black scarf
thrown in the air
Two camps of evil blood
fight on this spot
where the soul should detach itself
In flight they draw a cross
Where shall I confine my weeping
Where shall I travel
A gypsy woman robs their souls
wraps them in tiny blue rags
and wades through the river
to conceal her tracks
Three gypsy children
three yellow marigolds

with half a soul in their bodies
are reading the stars
Bury them in warm sand
to guard them from cold
I hear two marching bands
The red foam gathers on my fingers
Why should I part them
Why should I kill them
when they were born at war
I sit in pavilions
adorned with cold poppies
You have spread out the rag
over the blue rock of thunder
while your children
were picking the red stalks of sorrel
thinking under which cloud to stop
and wait for the dew
A dream
but in that dream you were interrupted
by the song of a sad owl
which pours out its gall
into a hollow tree

I've buried them in the garden
Where shall I confine my weeping
where shall I travel
A red and black rooster
fight in the sky

Simic & Mihailovich

OWL

You ought to live in the mountains
to weep after the summits
What do you want in the city attics
You, phosphorous and dark bird from god knows where

You fly in the moonlight slow as a century
which seeks the lost jewels from the sky
The dry wind has withered your wings
Your love is spent and now you can't fly
where your voice went O when I return to the city
with a blade of grass to keep me company
you wait for me with the chorus of owls in darkness
Nothing else is left for us but
To weep at night for what we've seen during the day.

Simic

THE ROAD TO THE MOUNTAIN

I will discover the red stone of thunder
O dried herbs
I will roll you into a cigar
and light you from the lightning
The sky-bird is an evil sign
Do not drink nocturnal water
my unshod horse
you will not carry me home
Because magic was buried with the foundation stone
                                              of my house
I tripped over subterranean winds
I will lie in the starry gardens on the hill
in a bed of roses
Let them light a candle on my head
and let the hail beat me flat as wheat
I was ready to take root
but my mole came
My unshod horse, you will drop dead from my weight
The cattle bar my way
The sky is scorched by lightning
The weeping stones rush towards my head
I won't reach home before the first cockcrow.

Mihailovich & Kizer

BRANISLAV PETROVIĆ 1937–

Born in 1937 in Bjeluša near Titovo Užice, Branislav Petrović has studied at the University of Belgrade and now works as a free-lance writer. His collections of poetry include *Moć govora* (Power of Speech, 1961), *Gradilište* (The Construction Site, 1964), and *O prokleta da si Ulico Rige od Fere* (Damn You, the Street Riga of Fera, 1970).

With Matija Bećković, Petrović represents a new voice in contemporary Serbian poetry. Ebullient, playful, and irreverent at times, using everyday speech and declamatory tones, and striving consciously for experimental and modernistic effects, he has become one of the leading poets of the Belgrade circle.

HOW I FELT AS THE PILOT OF THE PLANE FROM WHICH ALBERT EINSTEIN WAS SCATTERED TO THE WINDS

Solemn, I felt solemn.
That wonderful old man, that handful of ashes.
The plane at full speed toward the stars,
a splendid machine, faultless instruments.

We move away from the earth, from his workrooms.
From his physics, from his poetry, from his dog.
Farewell little girl with whom last spring,
under a false name,
I dined
under the limes!
Albert,
uncle Albert, wave to the little girl!

He can't.
Reduced to his true dimensions.
Like a well-written composition:
concise.

You understand?
ALBERT EINSTEIN
not like a packet of pudding!

I hold the handle I control the instruments,
the wings of the plane are my wings,
the machine the most excellent make rights itself
and now we fly slowly
parallel to his earth to his dream,
to his temporary dwelling place.

Some boys, down on the earth, run after us,
(they fly bravely)
It all reminds one of spraying mosquitoes
in the marshy suburbs.
I am not a philosopher,
I am not a farm worker—
I am an ordinary pilot—
and yet,
I am in excellent control of my nerves;
but,
when the employees of the undertakers
opened the tiny chest,

and when the dust blew away,
like the death of a little bird,
when the world blew away!—
if there were no bottles of gin,
my friends,
anything could happen!

How did I feel?
Well how would you feel?

Williams

POEM ABOUT ANA'S RETURN FROM THE SUMMER HOLIDAY

My little gypsy has returned from the sea sunburnt
sunburnt as an African queen what
do I care if she kissed some lout
from Pančevo down at the sea now
it is important that she has come back to me for
at the sea there are dangerous sharks there are
sailors at the sea there are
fishermen at the sea someone
might have taken her knees from me
for a monument in his town
pirates might layabouts
might have stolen her from me tell
me what the sea looks like has
the sea a younger brother is
the sea against the war does
the sea like barrels of fresh beer does
the sea know how to swim how
do the french kiss little gypsy
my beloved my
wife?

Williams

★ ★ ★

There is no longer any darkness which I have not descended
                    searching for my gold.
Naked and poor I am falling into abyss.
Everything familiar and dear I have exchanged for unknown
celebrating my destruction in advance.

It's all right for a mason: when he is bothered he builds houses.
It's even more so for a doctor: when he is ill he treats people.
It is hardest for me my pure love—
words are deserting me in droves.

Mihailovich

THE SECOND PART OF GUN JOKES

IV

Constellations!
I have been staring at the sky for two hours already.

And it is late, time for sleep,
but the head is not returning from above.

Mihailovich

THE CONQUEST OF AUSTRALIA

XXIV

The creator is visiting his abysses
the sun is his torch.

When he enters the region of man
there is a sight to behold:
nothing is as he has foreseen,
nothing is as he has left.

Mihailovich

MATIJA BEĆKOVIĆ 1939–

Matija Bećković was born in 1939 in Senta. He studied Yugoslav literature at the University of Belgrade, and now lives as a professional writer.

Since 1961 he has published several books of verse: *Vera Pavladoljska* (1961), *Metak lutalica* (A Vagabond Bullet, 1963), *Tako je govorio Matija* (So Spake Matija, 1966), and *Reče mi jedan čoek* (A Man Told Me, 1970). He has also written drama and TV plays. One of these, *Che* (1969), has been published in English.

Bećković is a poet of unusual originality, sharp wit, boldness, and topical satire. He often evokes the old heroic ways of his native Montenegro and employs its racy language, which is slowly disappearing. His socially conscious poetry, his original and deliberate selection of anti-poetic images, and his sense of humor, give him a definite kinship with other Eastern European poets like Miroslav Holub and Tadeusz Rozewicz. The Villonesque emotional climate of his poems has had an influence on young Serbian poets.

TWO WORLDS

Soon now that day has to come:
We'll mail petitions to all the wardens

To save us from fear freedom winter
And allow us to serve our time.

And when they finally throw us in chains,
Let the world lose its shameful balance,

So that between the two halves that make the world,
The convict's half becomes the bigger one,

And the guards out of shame and fear
One night plead to stay with us.

Simic

NO ONE WILL WRITE POETRY

No one will write poetry any more.
The immortal themes will abandon the poems
Unhappy with the way they were understood and versified.
Everything that was once subject of poetry
Will rebel against it and its cowardice,
Objects themselves will express what the poets had no
    courage to say.
Sea—the ancient theme of poets will leave poetry forever
And return to its grave where it grew up.
The sunset—turned ridiculous,
The starry sky—driven into a cliché,
Will forsake poetry.
The roses will insist on their color
And will not agree to the fickleness of poets.
Word *freedom* will escape and return to its meaning.
Poets will have no language in which to sing.
No one will stand between the poet and his poetry,
And so poems will attack poets
Demanding that they fulfill their promises.
The poets will retreat from all that they've said,
But everything that they imagined and prophesied will
    catch up with them.
Poetry will demand their lives
So that its metaphors may remain true and irrefutable.
In generations to come
No one for any price will want to be a poet.

Future poets will have better ways of spending their time.
The free man will not consent to write poems
    in order to be a poet—
And yet there's no other way to be a poet.
A tree—yesterday's symbol in poetry
Will wail from the square of its dark past
And no one will be able to equal its lament
Since it knows itself better than anyone else.
True poets will be against poetry
And all over the world they'll have the same thought:
For the sake of its esteem in the eyes of true poets,
No one will write poetry anymore.

Simic

IF I KNEW I'D BEAR MYSELF PROUDLY

If I knew I'd bear myself proudly
Before judges and serving my sentence,
What a trail I'd blaze and endure everything,
Warding it all off with my bare limbs.

If I knew I'd kick the table alone
Under my feet and fix the noose myself,
My soul would earn itself eternity
And my hangman go on weeping after me.

But I'm afraid, I'd start to beg,
To sob, to kneel, to betray everything,
Just to save my bare ass,
I'd spit on all and agree to everything.

Simic

BOGOMIL GJUZEL 1939–

Bogomil Gjuzel, a graduate in English literature from Skopje University, is a Macedonian poet of exceptional promise. He has translated extensively from both English and French, and now works for television and theater.

His books of verse are *Medovina* (Mead, 1962), *Alhemiska ruža* (Alchemist Rose, 1963), *Nebo, Zemlja, Sunce* (Sky, Land and Sun, 1963), and *Mironosci* (The Peacebringers, 1965).

He is a contemplative poet with close ties to his native soil. With him we witness the beginnings of a conscious effort to organize the particular Macedonian experience and sensibility. His poems impress by their formal excellence, and the evocative and sensuous quality of his language.

HOMAGE TO STONE

Stone, you that for ages fell in love with the dust
stone, you that cure yourself falling
and still ail for the sky
you, who reject to serve anyone
gnawed by poverty
covered with pleadings, scratched with nails
worn out by bare feet
caressed in despair to bring you to life
thrown so that you may circle like a bird
around the thought until it turns to stone
tinkered with heartbeats as with a hammer
and still dumb mute
proud hard obstinate stone.

You who sacrificed both death and life
for a fiercer existence
you who rejected the temporal presence

you who were once a plant, an animal and a man
but returned to your primeval being
near the beloved dust,
you who brought strife into space
you who made .e elements quarrel
you who imprisoned the light
you who lure us into your permanence
terrifyingly indifferent to the uninitiated—
go burst with the seed of dynamite
burst with my bad wish
proud hard obstinate stone.

You were always the unavoidable nothing
you mocked fire the stench of water
you lied to the earth
made the highest peak equal
to the depths of the abyss
you who toy with gravity
fall and get up again
in order to suffer more
where is one to find for you a peaceful depth?
Levitating incurably in the river of life
you'll be without rest
proud hard obstinate stone.
You who like a ball break the lightnings
raise the barricade of comprehension
you who pass like flooding lava
through the rotten door of the senses
and thrown by my muscular catapult
drop in the empty space of unwritten poetry
you who like Moloch melt down the darkness
throwing the sparks of rust into the light
you who crumbled Saints' halos
together with softened skulls
you who steadily dismantle the skeleton of air
you who will not admit a tear
until the whole eye flows out
sizzling like a hot drop of metal

incomprehensible ugly and divine
proud hard obstinate stone.

You who straighten beauty's bones
like to a sweet woman that has no choice
but to offer herself to you
to be sucked out like a beehive,
you who dealt with the ages
we now only mention
as with a pack of snotty brats
you who assaulted the stars
until you taught them to keep their distance
you who ground down the gods
rolling them through a dry stream bed
and then slyly permitted them
to borrow for themselves your flesh
what evil what malice to you
mean vile foul exiled stone.

Simic

SULTRINESS

I
Those deep wounds in the sky,
the lightnings, bear no fruit.
Only a bloody slaughterhouse remains
like a battlefield after the attack.

And the rain that falls brings no fruit,
only the headless corpses of the newborn dead,
and the house has turned transparent
like a phantom, an empty sheet of paper,
like a mouse scared out of its wits that rushes
straight into the mouth of the cat, History.

No help at all from the sound of thunder

which plays jokes with our ears,
only a still deeper division grows
in the gorge of the bottomless pain.

II

Light is forbidden
The lightnings have become subterranean rivers of fire—
of the arch of current between two poles.

The stars are lost fireflies
which the heavy air draws
to bring illness into the root
and thus enflamed spread the seed, if at all.

The ash finally nourishes us all,
bread-stone which crumbles from satiety.

Reid & Simic

THE DAGGER OF BEAUTY

I

Is this a time of hatred
or the seasonal change heralded by doves?
If spring is coming I grow still uglier
in the mirror of droughts and barren years
and my love will again gallop away
on a herd of wild horses from before my gates,
gates which are still buried deep in snow.

Now my ugliness plunders the chambers
and I make the whole house creep.
The master is out hunting for signs,
hunting for new seed and new blood.
She is in her bridal chamber
spinning and falling asleep over her beauty
but soon my shadow will swallow her.

Oh, you are too far off, master, to see
how she forgets herself combing her hair before the mirror.

With my yellow thumb I open the window
looking for the gypsies to come
selling poisoned combs and ugly mirrors
looking for weddings with new-found weapons
but the time offers only the wind's keen dagger
a time of love and hate.

II

My thought is thawing. Outside
the young black earth is sprinkled
with the blood of roosters. Still
the master, the man of the sacred woods,
is not here. I can't hide from the white dawn
or the dagger given me by this time,
nor from the gypsies who peer through the windows
loaded with poisonous gifts
nor from the armed weddings
which have their scimitars.
She is in her chamber spun into her beauty's dream
menaced by my shadow before her door.

My dagger is great from hatred
and can't be hidden from the white portals.
It will crawl through the pitch black woods of night
to cut the thread of her dream,
my master's beautiful dagger
who hunts hopelessly for his seed and blood.

The night is full of fresh green woods. This night.
Her door is quite eaten by dreams
and cannot stop my solid shadow.
Tenderly I creep beneath her silks
and bridal dress. She is beautiful, warm
in the lamplight, unspun in her dream.
But my dagger of white dawn is even more beautiful!

I cut off her head, that ball
of unspun dreams. The dagger sang
softly over her throat and vanished in the dawn,
the dawn that lopped the fresh green woods of night.
My shadow razed her chamber.

Well, master, come now to kiss your blood
which gave you no manhood in the hunt.

III

Her head blossomed in the heat of a May day
and, like a torch of dreams yet unspun,
gives the chambers a shuddering light. The house is razed.
The gypsies and the weddings trampled it down in their
        spring raid.

Now she is more fair. Fairer than death.
O, how I love her! That red hair of hers
woven from the fibre of the East, where her blood
paints the landscape of the hunt for male seed.
At last her beauty has slain the time
and emptied the hourglasses on the steppes
where men roam awakening the woods.
My ugly shadow has vanished.

Only the child's cry in her chamber
was severed by my dagger sharpened by the dawn.
That second night I sacrificed my milk
which could have suckled whole tribes
that each morning and evening trampled over the roof.
I will not give birth from love. I buried
the old year's seed under the very threshold if I remember
                          right

awaiting news from the master
who has ordered all this in his thoughts.

IV

I hunger after you, master, in the full moon.
Wormwood sprang up on the threshold for snakes to litter
there
that neither the gypsies nor the armed weddings might cross.
The locusts came and the summer plague
to harm the old year's seed with disease.
Her head rotted away in the noontide
and melted in the hot evenings. Her beauty
remained alone in the house free to multiply with worms.
Now only I walk outside in the night fields
leaving behind the hallowed home
and the stale bread buried in ashes. The dog
howls in the distance. I am alone
all the time fighting this beauty,
waiting for you. This powerful body of mine
will be impregnated neither by draughts nor a thousand barren
years,
without you new seed from this year's hunt.
Come, my master, I starve for you!

The doves died and the summer brought death.
The house is bound with the chains of draught.
My ugly shadow is left to roam the convents.

V

Let worse befall me! Alas, the hunt failed.
He came that morning when I gossiped of my beauty
to the dagger, on a dying horse, with a perished falcon,
he came ashen and pale from the thought of the failed hunt.
He said: it's still the same, and asked for his bride.
Softly singing to it I showed my dagger.

He called the servants caressing me with his whip.
Let worse inflict me, for the hunt was a failure
and the new seed not brought. And while I waited for the servants
I sang to my dagger the soft familiar song of beauty,
for he was not that master from before the last hunt;

Gjuzel • 215

his hopeless thoughts of new seed had devoured him.
But he was a better singer. He brought the servants with
                                                    torches
and said again: it will still be the same, and crushed
                                        the wormwood
setting the old stone on the threshold. The wormwood sap
                                            burst into song.

The servants took out their knives, singing tortured
by the hopeless hunt. Let the worst befall me,
for the new seed was not brought.
I threw away the dagger calling for four horses.

They brought four horses. I bound them to my body,
and sang to all the points to tear apart my beautiful body,
my beautiful body to all four points.

The horses pulled, and died, but sang!

Reid & Gjuzel

PROFESSIONAL POET

The last word, the last hasty swallow

you get up from the table, after your working day
and catch the first bus to the kitchen
you tear off a hunk of bread, inhale the good oven odors
Your body, leaden with weariness, the mold
you stuff with rich food
switch on the set
                    and inspect the back yard
through another screen
                                with a wet finger
you flip the pages of the sky.

Nothing will come of nothing.
                              Clematis tendrils
float in the void . . . THEY MUST BE TRAINED ON A TRELLIS
your daughter brings a chair for you
The table is set, your wife calls
through the window of a parallel world.

After dinner, you walk in the garden
alone in your pressurized space-suit,

                                   stars all around you
even beneath you. Your antennae must be redirected
The pear tree, newly pruned, requires manure.

Back to the module:
                   Daddy, what does it mean
to be a monster?
                   Suddenly, the chain of command dissolves
bits of paper whirling in free fall
around the table:
                   untouched paper
and your pencil, ominous as a revolver.

Kizer

DOJČIN'S AGONY

Savage is the law decreeing you be born alone
And alone fashion the doom that brings destruction.
But yet more dreadful is to be confounded
By the snare of unborn fruit.
If mother and country were not damned by us,
They would return our malediction twofold.

And so I lie in a tower of air
Thick-swaddled in folds of mist and snow,
Expecting the day that fate has promised
When I will unlock the world with a new damnation

And tense for the last blow.
I waited for the light that would save me,
Tunneled through the night of my parents.

I stepped on wonder-working springs and grasses,
Fouled my weapons with smears of blood,
And again I lie in Pain in the White City, the bitter city,
And again, nothing will come to pass . . .

Champe

TOMAŽ ŠALAMUN 1941–

One of the youngest poets in this anthology, Tomaž Šalamun was born in 1941 in Zagreb. With his several books of poetry—*Poker* (Poker, 1966), *Namen pelerine* (The Purpose of the Cloak, 1968), *Romanje za Maruško* (Pilgrimage for Maruško, 1971), *Bela Itaka* (White Ithaca, 1972), and *Amerika* (America, 1972)—he has already moved to the forefront of contemporary Slovenian poetry. His poems have been translated into several languages.

Šalamun's poems have an associative quality which gives the impression of automatic writing. What keeps them together and gives them their inevitability, is Šalamun's keen sense of the organic nature of the poem with all its verbal and lyrical connotations. Consequently, the "chaos" is a ruse, a freeing agent, for his poems never fail to drive their meaning home. With his creative freedom and adventurousness, Šalamun, along with a few other contemporary poets, initiates a new era in Slovenian poetry.

PEACE TO THE PEOPLE OF THIS EARTH

God remembers all the travelers
        remembers the rain in Arras
        and David's son
remembers a squirrel falling down on to the ground
        I yell rabbits
thinking those really are rabbits because I'm myopic
        God remembers Stavrogin
churns of rotting wood and our games
        the way I clean my teeth
        and say peace to the people of this earth
the only thing I like about Empire-style furniture
        are the Empire-style legs
        God remembers

God remembers how painstakingly I worked
to fashion a tetrahedron out of a slice of bread
then kept throwing it furiously against the wall
and there was the war
and others ate saccharine
the fire is getting closer

night of whiskers

I see hell where my angel used to stand

Šalamun & Hollo

HOMAGE TO A HAT & UNCLE GUIDO & ELIOT

Just like Clay became a world champion
because there was something wrong with his leg
I'll be a great poet
because they double-crossed me
with Frank's blue cap
sent for Christmas 1946
and since then I've left him out of prayers
song of songs of pansalamunian religion
terribly democratic people's institution
which takes in everything
from stamps biscuits Tzilka, Horak, Parmesan
to that poor idiot
who drank his hotel away in Vetimiglia
and faded out somewhere in the world
just like our prayers fade out
its last important reformer was uncle Guido
known among the folks
for his invention of a new pipe for a steamboiler
but that was not his main occupation
his main thing was
watering flowers
just like Spinoza

a bit taller though
meditating on and off on death
buying us ice cream
each day made new
that was between
magnolia Brandenburg & America

two days ago Eliot died
my teacher

Šalamun & Hollo

JONAH

how does the sun go down?
like snow
what color is the sea?
wide
jonah are you a flag?
I'm a flag

let all glow-worms rest

what are stones like?
green
how do puppies play?
like poppies
jonah are you a fish?
I'm a fish
jonah are you a sea-urchin?
I'm a sea-urchin
listen to the rustle

jonah is suppose a reindeer runs through the forest
jonah is suppose I look at the mountain breathing
jonah is suppose all the houses
do you hear suppose a rainbow?

what's the dew like?
are you asleep?

Šalamun & Anderson

RASPBERRIES ARE II

We arrive in Karlovac
and we discuss
what tactics to use
man to man
double center
or cross formation

and Guato's got new sneakers
and the lights go on
and everybody has his number
and Skinko is a fantastic guard
and they take time-out
but nobody breaks into our zone
and all our baskets are boneless without touching

then in the second half aunt Agatha comes
and says
oooh
    oooh how pleased I am
and aunt Lela comes
and says
oooh
    oooh how pleased I am
and Olivieri comes
and says
oooh
    oooh how pleased I am
Derin
Camerlengo

siora Pesaro
and they all walk up and down in the stands
and sing
oooh
        oooh how pleased we are
and you
are you pleased with yourself
they ask me
when I throw the ball back in

and I think

of course
I'm pleased
of course I'm pleased
oooh
        ooooh how pleased I am

at the end the reporters ask me
why did you lose the game

raspberries are
raspberries I say

Taufer & Scammell

★ ★ ★

one day in the dining room I took the exact measurements
of the distance from the lower lefthand corner of the picture to the floor
and the distance from the lower righthand corner to the floor
as I had the persistent feeling that the picture was hanging
one day I realized there is dolphin roe
one day I took the suspenders out of the closet
one day it said in the papers
the King of Cambodia would return our visit
one day I thought who'll be the first one to count up to a million

one day I went out in the street to get some exercise
I walked on the righthand side of the sidewalk
one day it occurred to me that every human being has to die
one day M. France bought a grove of birchtrees
from a young artist because it occurred to him
that you have to take risks to get into the money
one day I bought pretzels although that is something I never do
because the dust lies on the street
one day St. Arnolfina appeared on the calendar
one day I said to myself why isn't my father great enough
then I would be great enough too

Šalamun & Hollo

LOOK, BROTHER

I am abandoning iconoclastic levels, I am a tiger
in a heart a seedbud the soul germinated in you, did she?
anima, brown sun of unterrestrial strata of roofs
immersed shadows, sheep squeezed in shelter
within palms, dramas
within reach of pack smell, among the petty lumber tradesmen
o light, asunder, excitement
eat fruit, peel the splendor of goods
the meadows are lacerated, the gazelles faster
morbidity, dark fingers, coffee's beauty
of ruins, femme, moments of gravitation
look brother, blotting-papers, dirty putrid chalets
he was walking in the land in the year of joy
coming to water, scooping it from the bottom
yielding to the eldest son, to the ship's designers
yielding to beautiful vistas, to the racism of the dream
burning madness of herbage, immanent soldiery
I see Cairo from the sky, I see triangle vomiting
the leader of snakes, Rudolph the Emperor's court
are you happy eating?
do you compare steadiness with the color of jute?

with deer rutting, blacks, olive branches?
a brocade, illuminated manuscripts, rise and fall of the family
little Romanies sit by
who's paying?
I am emanating, we are usurping Jerusalem
eating corn mush with wooden spoons
ceiling and trunk, kneeling, cementing the walls
we pour seed in front of the t.v. camera
will you stand up? will you wake up? will you sing hymns?
we were plowing, preparing firewood for the summer
no need for peace, no need for suns, no need for sorrow
the thighs are resting, Romany
thighs are tired and tremble
the hot blue blood is cut
even before night, even before raging warlocks

Šalamun & Hollo

WHO IS WHO

Tomaž Šalamun you are a genius
you are wonderful you are a joy to behold
you are great you are a giant
you are strong and powerful you are phenomenal
you are the greatest of all time
you are the king you are possessed of great wealth
you are a genius Tomaž Šalamun
in harmony with all creation we have to admit that
you are a lion the planets pay homage to you
the sun turns her face to you every day
you are just everything you are Mount Ararat
you are perennial you are the morning star
you are without beginning or end
you have no shadow no fear
you are the light you are the fire from heaven
behold the eyes of Tomaž Šalamun
behold the brilliant radiance of the sky

behold his arms behold his loins
behold him striding forth behold him touching the ground
your skin bears the scent of nard
your hair is like solar dust
the stars are amazed who is amazed at the stars
the sea is blue who is the sky's guardian
you are the boat on high seas that no wind no storm can destroy
you are the mountain rising from the plain the lake in the desert
you are the speculum humanae salvationis you hold back the forces of
    darkness
beside you every light grows dim beside you every sun appears dark
every stone every house every crumb every mote of dust
every hair every blood every mountain every snow
every tree every life every valley every chasm
every enmity every lamb every glow every rainbow

Šalamun & Hollo

MILORAD PAVIĆ 1929–

Milorad Pavić was born in Belgrade, where he studied Yugoslav literature at the University of Belgrade and later received a doctorate in comparative literature at the University of Zagreb. He has been active in editorial offices and publishing houses. He now works at Belgrade's leading publishing house *Prosveta*.

His poetic output includes only two books of verse: *Palimpsesti* (Palimpsests, 1967) and *Mesečev kamen* (The Moon Stone, 1971). Pavić also translates and writes literary criticism and history. His recent history of Serbian literature of the baroque period was hailed as a major academic achievement. A handful of his poems was published in the United States in *Four Yugoslav Poets*.

In his poetry, Pavić attempts to answer the questions of present-day existence by going back to the old historical myths. The medieval, baroque, and modern periods are synthesized in his poetry, exhibiting similar, if not identical, problems and dilemmas. A traditionalist, Pavić is also a modern poet in that he refuses to separate our time from the near and distant past.

GREAT SERBIAN MIGRATION 1690

On Sunday we buried the icons
   except for one milk-tasting
   that weeps with eyes of its breasts
   and feeds with starry tear

On Sunday we walled our books into the tower
   except for one that can be read in the mirror of holy water
On Sunday we tied the birds into bells to ring after us
   but the bell of our Despot we took along

   since his word it utters when upside-down it tolls
On Sunday we scattered the monks over the province
   except for the one who understood the holy bell

We took him on our ship to divide the message of our Despot
and at black cock's crowing we prayed for southern wind
and received what we prayed for and at white cock's crow
we regretted what we asked for

For each bird that flies over the river
is the bridge for our thoughts
and every butterfly a letter to our eyes,
While here we dwell deprived of our homeland

and find no bridge back to ourselves
Wild apples tumble as though horses pass in a gallop
through a garden
while birds' feathers burn in flight and throughout the night
but we don't care
whether we will understand the words of holy books
frozen above the river

when they thaw and thunder again
and the name of holy Despot is pronounced again
by the bell
Like a shield we raise the icon with salt-eyes pure with tears

On her we see only the earth's black winds
black bulls in the offing, where they graze the foam
off the waves
where they graze flying-fish.

Simic

from HOLY MASS FOR RELJA KRILATICA

First Song

Rejoice you who sleep with a finger in your ear
Good tidings will come to you
For you are the one who tied a knot in his own moustache
So not to forget your name
Wrote in the palm of the hand the origin and destination
    of your journey
You are fear that reared up on its hind legs
And let its sideburns and beard grow
You are hoarse seeking the right word in the whirlwind of silence
Between your eyes' paths darkness thickens for you
And between your teeth laugher which you find
    harder and harder to remember
For its reins are not in your hands
You laugh in the direction in which others pull the moustache
Carry your soul in the nose and they teach you how to sneeze
You'll tie another knot one name in each moustache
Neither Relja to the Serbs nor Hariton to the Greeks.

Third Song

But I'm the one to whom others spit in the hand when he works
And in the plate when he eats
The one who failed to warm his chair
The eater of knives and darkness
From one mad rock to another I leap
While one leg wishes no good to the other
I eat with a penny under my tongue
With tears and sweat I salt my bread
In one pocket wheat grows for me in the other grass
Rain falls in my bowl and snow in my bed
I'm the one who combs himself with a fork
The one who plants knives and fattens his teeth
Since spoons do not grow bigger while I eat
They gave me wine inside a bell
If I drink it doesn't toll if it tolls I don't drink.

Pavić • 229

Fourth song

Rejoice bather between two waters
For you are the one who forgot where the earth's navel is
You stepped on someone's robe in the dark
They beat you by the clock and plant a hair in your egg
While you yawn into the flute
Steal God's days and devour them:
To the first that comes you bite off an ear or a finger
At night you are the one who practices gardening
You plow your shadow and water it with sweat
You planted the root of an ancient word
And grass grew on your tongue
Thus you guard yourself not to utter *above* or *below*
Nor *cold* nor *hot* nor *East* nor *West*
When you grow hoarse with your dumbness
You'll spit into the candle and die
Neither ours in what you have nor yours in what we have.

Fifth Song

But I'm the one who carries a garlic clove in the ear
My head in the sack my brain beyond the sea
I stuck a gold coin in my bread
And let the bread float down the river
I turned the eyes of rings in my hand and go begging
My river is full of apples my waters flower twice
My day breaks until noon from noon on it sets
Master of sundials and moon-clocks
I water unless the great royal highways
Disappear from under my feet
For the years wane behind the hills
And my day grows cold my honesty old
They've salted my fire domesticated my fork
And teach me to bring the moonrock in my teeth
While I piss in my shadow and make supper for my clock
Plant fish and mean to harvest hair
Neither a sackful of days nor handful of years

Sleep is my older brother and illness my older sister
Bite me into the tongue if they don't outlive me
And I neither sipped nor blew nor ate nor broke into crumbs.

Sixth Song

Rejoice singer of songs for the deaf
For you are the one we stick a crown under the hat
They gave you two tamed shadows
To lie in one and cover yorself with the other
You answer to bread and water and travel blind
They strung your *gusla* with ravenous manes
They taught you our sorrow and weeping
Burdened the horse with the icon of Saint Paul
Whipped him hard under you
Alone ate the grass of forgetting that wipes out all memory
And thus forgot the name of their milk
And by what seed they were sown
We tell you—a careful man hunter of elusive dreams
Can even out of the night bring sweet water in his mouth
But you are the one whose tongue has a bad chill
Whose family name grows hoarse with silence
When you get thirsty you'll drink up the darkness
Die under a foreign fruit tree and with a foreign name
Neither a magi to yourself nor to us a prophet.

Seventh Song

Rejoice eleventh finger reckoner of stars
For you are the one exiled into the light
Your mind is made up with angelic speed
While the wings were given to you to catch him
We threw him on heaven's shores like a crown
To listen to the moon's breathing
Where he falls down we'll build a house
Go now and bring him back
In a sleeve full of moonlight
We are teaching you to bear God's beard

To crawl out among the stars
Like a worm from an iron walnut into the flesh of the wind
But you sit in your heart above all nights and fish
We teach you to spit into the point of galactic balance
Between the pull of the moon and the pull of the earth
But you've caught the mole of heavens
Sowed feathers in her back
And wait for the wings to sprout
You teach her to tell time
Terrestial time makes her hiccup
Neither your last name's name nor your first name's nickname.

Eighth Song

But I'm the one whom they stole a button from his trouser leg
The one who keeps a finger in the bottle instead of a cork
Priest of a god with two suns I bow down to two easts
And they teach me to steal my cap
Servant of two masters I stand on one leg
There where it thundered last year
I keep an eye on royal highways
Whether they join on the hill
With a wooden bell I count the horsemen on this side
For the knowledge of those beyond the hill and viceversa
When I make an error confusion follows and they both run
But they stole a button from my trouser leg
And I keep the finger in the bottle instead of a cork
Neither tzar's own nor king's or shepherd's nor hunter's dog.

Ninth Song

Rejoice mason of years
For you are the one who builds a house for your hours
Keeps night in the mouth and grazes the clouds with the eyes
They've cut your hair under the pot
In the shape of the Greek letter *omega*
And you don't know how to read it
Only paupers and lepers bow down to it

For you are the one who with an anchor plows islands in the sky
And gathers beautiful places into a column
A moonrock you've planted under the pillow
You weep with tears of wine and water it
One day and perhaps even earlier
A flying city will grow
Constantinople neither in heaven nor on earth
You'll lock it so the angels can't get in
Instead of icons you'll place all of us there
Let him who can't get in be envious
Of the one who can't come out
We'll pull your shadow from under your feet
Bury it in the water
You won't have a place to land if you return
Neither Relja to the Serbs nor Hariton to the Greeks.

Simic

MIRKO MAGARAŠEVIĆ 1946–

The youngest poet in this anthology, Mirko Magaraševic is a representative of a new, sophisticated, and intellectually oriented approach in contemporary Serbian poetry. Although he is still studying medicine at the University of Belgrade, he has published two collections of poems: *Pogoci za vučje i druge oči* (Hits for the Wolf's and Other Eyes, 1969) and *Povorke trougla* (The Parades of the Triangles, 1971).

Magaraševic endeavors to create his own set of myths based on the world of animals in order to use them as symbols for various aspects of human existence. He lends to this modern fable writing a cool cerebral analysis of our everyday thoughts and actions. A demanding poet, he continues to develop his own style and personal vision.

THE WOLF'S EYES

While the dawn falls in the middle of the cave
transforming the secret toys of the world
into the messages of light—
he is already far away.
Despising human values
he gallops in gracious steps
                    of his hunger
In the evening he declares that the mountain
is his planetarium
in which the foot and the shoe are not
                        welcome.

Over night he sharpens his knives
for that hour before dawn
promising his she-wolf
that he will not be too violent,
that he will give advantage

to those in cottages
hoping that they will be again the first
to make a mistake
and provoke laughter under his forehead.
Therefore he feels like a mountain wind
when he passes through the gates
                              of the out-foxed reason,
quieting them with his slaughtering assault
and the steam of blood on the snow.
With a cat's jump he advances through the woods
across the scales of past autumn
searching for a tame dinner in the valley.

It sometimes happens that they twist his neck
but he does not regret much
because then he moves over into his killer.

Then he goes on multiplying
                    in men's own eyes.

Magaraševič & Mihailovich

THE WOLF'S JAWS IN OUR HEARTS

    Behind our backs
far away
    the wolf's jaws are combing
discords in our hearts.

In front of mirrors
    we perfect good-natured smiles
picking from our teeth the leftovers
    of inborn bloodthirst.

We hate the dignity of strength
    enviously piercing the days,
stringing them like pearls
    on the wolf's luxuriant chest.

Each of us believes that in his chest
        speak the best voices
and dark blood streams most purely,
        but there, in place of a proud heart

        a shivering dwarf
crouches, picking flowers
        off the steep meadows
of fear.

        Let us forget
that we are hunted wolves
        whose ribs at birth were broken.
Our dreams will be more peaceful.

Magarašević & Mihailovich

CAT'S DRIVE

Galloping across the yard,
I run up a tree
he was chasing me with fire
in his eyes;
and when he reached me and stretched his paw
without hiding the face of his intent
I bristled up my fur
pretending reluctance:
            that was the only way to
            attract his desire.
Then it became all the same to me.

Now, I stretch my claw in the new seed
skimming the fur on the other side
            of the mind.

Magarašević & Mihailovich

AHMED MUHAMED IMAMOVIĆ 1944–

Ahmed Muhamed Imamović was born in Sarajevo and attended university there, studying mechanical engineering and modern painting. He is the author of four collections of poems, including *Writer on a Motorcycle* (1972), and *First Signs of Life* (1975), and has also written for a popular television series. Imamović has won several prizes, among them the Laurel Wreath of Goran in 1975, and has exhibited widely as a painter.

IF I EVER DIE BUT THAT WILL BE SOON

Findings are incorrect.

The trains are not late anymore
but they have completely ceased to arrive
And railway cars, tracks and conductors
are of no use to anything any more.

Some occupations are dying out
like dinosaurs.

Mental hospitals are being renovated
and are expanding considerably
New nurses are being employed
and highly qualified locksmiths
and welders
Are installing thick bars
on windows
with flowers
in the vases of abandoned skulls
While through long halls
brains are wandering without protection of any kind
I am traveling with a bouquet of roses in neglected forests
and finding the closest friends
on the branches

in natural shelter
among normal beasts
and birds.

Camomile
and clover
Embracing me
and kissing.

Bears and wolves
are pouring water out to me
to wash my hands
at the entrance to the main hunting ground.

Strawberries
hedgehogs
and squirrels
Conducting me
to the pleasant company
of chlorophyll
and unusually healthy mice.

Pieces of beef
and plucked hens
from a shop window
are writing registered letters to me:
All wards are welcome, physicians are
sold out a thousand years in advance and are
already sick themselves and are dying at their
posts saving their patients . . .

I am reading the letters
to the wild goats throughout the forest.

To the wild goats
which eat pages of paper
like tasty leaves

of the apple
and the pear.

Imamović & Branka Imamovic

PLAGUE OF KORNAT

Lay down your probing head
on The Plague of Kornat
and record the case in the books.

The case of someone who was sitting by the sea
with ears raised up above the North Star
waiting for more than seventy years.

One day
he disappeared he did not exist any more nobody saw him anywhere.

His disappearance was recorded by all stations
by unintelligible signs
at an unreachable and distant place.

Unreachable over a hundred million
Distant about three hundred million.

Into the constellation where we have lost him
fire is burning
on which his soul is being comfortably kept warm.

There is no light
there is no dark
to confuse him unusually immensely.

There is no air
that he has to breathe
There is no water
that he has to drink

There is no bread
that he has to eat.

He is neither dead
nor alive
He does not care about it.

Cities on the Earth
and villages
are for him a fantasy.
History and philosophy
foreign languages
and electricity
Make no sense.

Eternity he has surpassed
He lives
much longer.

He lives from the very beginning
when dispute about eternity first started.

Imamovíc & Branka Imamovíc

IN THE PLEASANT WORLD OF RATS AND DAMPNESS

Do you have any kind of doors
install them and fix them in place
Not to hear Them
not to see Them.

Any kind of doors
as long as they are doors
Their closing system to be functioning well
but their opening system to be easy to break
by help of simple mechanism to close them
and not to open them any more.

Not to hear Them how They hear Themselves
not to see Them how They see Themselves.

With Their sounds
made of empty cans
In Their clothes
made of spotted cellophane.

Let us tie around our necks
washed ties
let us put on our pants from dry cleaners
Let us throw away the receipts which were given for service
when we carried away our watches
to be repaired
And let us close the doors with excellent mechanism
to prevent those who are with us
inside
from coming from outside.

Close the doors
and order one door more from the fat repairman
secure yourself with locks
and security devices
when you will be asleep with a sweet dream
that They do not come to you to have tea and biscuits without rights.

Move yourself into the basement space
live with the rats
and with dampness
in the pleasant world of rats and dampness.

Don't allow Them to knock at your doors
order doors without knocking
Invincible
thick doors
can help you
only those
Doors which are still being perfected

and are produced one by one
by very complicated tools in the open space.

Hammer in thick boards
on the slot made for the small letter that we expect to come
and make children's boats
of the paper
which you were keeping for the answers.

Make children's boats
and let them go through the drainpipes
let them be small submarines.

Live off doors
on their inner side
Bite them
eat
drink them
Lose your weight because of them
and gain your weight because of them
Cultivate them
warm yourself on them
and shiver close beside them.

Die
but do not revive memories
of an elevator
which brought you where you are
of a traveling companion
and tomato juice.

Only sometime
so that you do not become mad
allow your friends to visit you
but let Them come in through other passageways
Those doors *do not open*.

Imamovíc & Branka Imamovíc